THE LIGHTSEEKER'S MANUAL

HOW TO COMMUNICATE WITH ANGELS, RAISE YOUR VIBRATIONS AND SAVE THE WORLD

A CHANNELED TEXT

HELENA CLARE

THE LIGHTSEEKER'S MANUAL
How to Communicate with Angels, Raise Your Vibrations
and Save the World
By HELENA CLARE
1. OCC032000 2. SEL032000 3. OCC003000
ISBN: 978-1-949642-49-0
EBOOK: 978-1-949642-50-6

Cover design by LEWIS AGRELL

Printed in the United States of America

Authority Publishing
11230 Gold Express Dr. #310-413
Gold River, CA 95670
800-877-1097
www.AuthorityPublishing.com

Contents

Prologue
by Helena Clare

Nothing about our lives is a coincidence. Before we incarnate we choose where we are born and who our parents will be, as well as close family and emotional relationships throughout life. That you have this book in your hand is unlikely to be mere chance. We have reached a critical moment in the world's history and you have an important role to play in the enlightenment of the Earth. You are ready for what waits in these pages.

After decades of hearing angels and wise spiritual beings in 2011 Source started communicating to me. It wasn't God tied to any single religion, but the Divine, the ultimate Truth, that crosses all religions. That is how s/he described itself.

The last few years have for many people been difficult. For me, since 2012 when *The Lightseeker's Manual* was communicated to me, life seems to have been one assault after another. Giving birth to a severely disabled child, quadriplegic and currently unable to talk with frequent life threatening episodes requiring hospitalisation, has meant I've had to value each precious moment with him, whilst financially planning his safety net if he outlives his parents. Facing financial challenges and exiting a destructive marriage have all been emotionally demanding. Experiencing all of this in South Africa, twelve thousand kilometres from the UK, where I am from, has added to the challenge, not to mention the backdrop of Covid and global economic and political strife.

Yet the words and practices of *The Lightseeker's Manual* have been so profound and powerful that I have been able to seize what I call *the platinum lining*, find the positive in all these steps and trust that these experiences are all given for the lessons they teach and enable me to share with others. It is only now that I feel ready to share the writings held within these covers, they are not mine to hide. Perhaps I had to go on this journey to be ready.

Most people believe in God but how do any of us prove God exists? My logical brain has demanded I prove this is the voice of Source, before I share it with the world, but there is no way to prove or disprove it. I've asked myself on so many occasions can this really be the voice of God. Yet the voice that came to me, calling itself Source or God, was so pure and wise, it was beyond my own knowledge. So I offer this book to the world, to let the words speak for themselves.

The Lightseeker's Manual is for open-minded people who want to contribute to improving the world through giving their own 'light' energy, both in meditation and in how they live their lives. It describes how God has made available thousands of celestial beings to work directly with people for their own healing and that of the planet. The Manual teaches people how to connect directly with angels and ascended humans, called ascended masters. It gives specific guidance on how people can Ascend (spiritually evolve) and how together we can help the world to Ascend to a Golden Age where all on the planet share in peace, prosperity, freedom and health and live in harmony with nature and the animal kingdom. It is very much a book about personal empowerment and empowerment of the world.

If you want to understand your life purpose on Earth and how you can save the world through the power of your own healing energy, by becoming a 'Lightworker', *The Lightseeker's Manual*, through meditations and exercises, reveals to you how.

Covid, environmental and political challenges have made us seek for an answer to 'What Next?' This book tells us part of the answer. Within these pages lies a miraculous adventure but also the strongest support you can ever imagine. It has helped me withstand tidal waves of trauma in my professional and personal life and remain joyful and steadfast. This support awaits you too.

Introduction: Message from Source

From I, from Source, from God, from Allah. I speak this in the name of truth, integrity and love. There is much you need to learn, beloveds. There is much that needs to change within this magnificent world. There is much damage that has been done. And there is much healing to be done.

The Earth is in balance. Not the balance of perfection, but a balance between decay and hardship on the one hand and a Golden Age on the other. I would like you to attain the Golden Age, and I have sent millions of helpers from the angelic kingdoms to enable the Earth to do this.

But humans, you have free will – free will not to ask for our help, free will to destroy the planet because of your greed toward each other and toward a never satisfied thirst for more, a *more* that will never make you happy. For happiness will only come when you realise you are connected to Me.

Through this Channel I have given you a Manual on how to raise your own vibrations to save the world and enable the planet Earth to attain the Golden Age. The Manual is easy to use and fun to follow, as joy is an essential part of raising your vibrations. But do not waste time. Do not defer reading this Manual and following the practices in this Manual for another year – for you do not have another year.

Much as I love every one of you and this beautiful planet, I can no longer tolerate what is becoming of your world. And so I ask you to receive this Manual as a gift to you, given out of My love for you. Read it, follow it, now.

With My love, God.

Chapter 1

RAISING YOUR VIBRATIONS IN ORDER TO ASCEND

This Manual is channelled from Me, God, Source, Allah. This is My Manual to help you Ascend – help you uplift the whole planet into a Golden Age, Heaven on Earth.

Many people who are reading this Manual will have spent their lives following Me through different religions. This Manual does not replace those religious books, but sits with them. For I do not belong to a single religion. I am all religions. I am the Source of All.

This Manual requires you to relinquish your need to be superior. By the end of this Manual, you will recognise the God-spark within you, and that you are equal to all and all are equal to you.

So how should you use this Manual? Read it over the course of the next six months, undertaking every visualisation and exercise. The Manual is slim and succinct, but profound. There is no extraneous information. Everything is important.

As a rough guide, I suggest working through one chapter every two weeks. I also suggest you repeat some exercises frequently, which is why at the end of each chapter you will find a corresponding two-week plan. Many of the exercises can be repeated every day. The Grounding and Protection must be repeated each morning and evening.

As you work your way through the Manual you will come into contact with Ascended Masters – highly evolved humans – such as Jesus, Prophet Mohammed and the Buddha. You may decide you resonate with a particular Ascended Master. To resonate more strongly and bring their qualities to you, there are certain mantras you can recite. These should be recited frequently throughout each day in order to increase the pace of your Ascension.

You will be given techniques to access three important energies, including the Mahatma and My own Source Energy. Initially, drawing the Mahatma Energy through your body should be repeated at least weekly, but it is an energy that can be used every day. At a certain point in the Manual, you will become ready to receive the Source Energy.

Please do not jump forward to the Source Energy because if you are not ready to receive it, it will do you no good – no harm, but no good. You must progress to a certain level to be able to receive My energy. The exercises in the chapters preceding the Source Energy chapter will allow you to reach that point.

Do not be harsh on yourself if you miss a week here and there; the Ascension process will simply take longer. Equally, do not think you can condense the process by skipping some of the exercises or visualisations. This Manual has been carefully constructed so there is nothing extraneous; even if you think you have worked through something previously, I urge you to perform every visualisation and exercise laid out here to ensure your Ascension is as fast as possible.

You will also notice that most of the exercises and visualisations focus on raising your own vibrations, rather than giving light to the world. This has been done on purpose so that by the time you reach the chapters where we teach you how to be light-workers, your vibrations are high enough to do the utmost good.

What do we mean by vibrations? In the celestial world, celestial beings vibrate at a very high frequency, a frequency so high and fast that, for most humans, they are not visible to the naked eye. Humans vibrate much more slowly. I ask you to raise your vibrations to let in the light. As you move up through the different dimensions to the seventh, your vibrations become closer to our own – *My* own – very fast vibration.

This does not mean that throughout the Manual you should not be beaming light to places, people or situations, to raise those vibrations; but the Manual has been purposefully constructed as a gradual process to raise your vibrations enough for you to be a significant light-worker in the world.

This Manual embodies the mysteries of the world. If you have wondered if there is more to life than what you have experienced so far, then you are absolutely correct. The world is mysterious and magnificent, just as I am. But in giving you this Manual, I invite you across the threshold of the mysterious and the magnificent. And I ask you to be part of it. I ask you to be part of enabling the Golden Age – enabling Heaven on Earth.

The Significance of 2012

2012 is a significant year in the calendar of many cultures. It is significant because the world is at a turning point, a turning point that can lead to a Golden Age if people work to raise their vibrations high enough. It is the end of a 26,000-year cosmic cycle. We're leaving the Age of Pisces and entering the Age of Aquarius. Everything lies in your hands.

The years after 2012 are all significant. Each year the actions of humans as a collective (averaged over the whole planet) will decide the course the world will take. Time is accelerated and effect is concentrated, so each action takes on greater weight than it did 100 years ago or more; it is more significant than even 5 years ago. So be aware of every move and action you take, every thought you have, and ensure they are carried out with the highest intention for the good of the planet.

Earth is a training ground – one of the most sought-after training grounds in the Universe. I have created this training ground with the celestial kingdom to enable Souls to learn and progress quickly along their spiritual paths.

It is sought after because it is very difficult. *Very challenging.* It presents unique challenges like those relating to sexuality and those created by the Veil of Amnesia adopted by all Souls who incarnate.

Before incarnation takes place, the Soul agrees which lessons they have to learn in that particular lifetime and Soul contracts are arranged with the beings around them – especially Souls who will be close relatives and friends – to allow them to learn those lessons. If those lessons are not learnt, they will return in another incarnation and learn them again, and so on until the vibrations of that Soul are high enough that they can eventually Ascend.

Ascension is where wisdom has been gained, spiritual wisdom embodied by love and light: *enlightenment.* Previously, I required Souls to reach the seventh dimension before they could Ascend from the planet Earth. The seventh dimension is the place where angels vibrate, as well as other celestial beings who work directly for Me and with Me. In the seventh dimension beings are pure love, and it is a magnificent place to exist in. Wonderful Masters like Buddha, Jesus, the Prophet Mohammed and Mother Mary, have reached the seventh dimension and work with us closely.

Recently I decided that for Souls on Earth to Ascend, they need not reach the seventh dimension but they could join us when they reached the sixth dimension. In the sixth dimension there are still many lessons to learn, but Souls have made significant progress in terms of loving unconditionally and committing their lives in some way to the betterment of the planet. I did this because I care for you so much, because by raising your own vibrations and reaching the sixth dimension, you will raise the vibrations of the Earth.

I also agreed that to Ascend, a Soul does not necessarily have to pass over and join Me in the celestial kingdom in the seventh dimension; rather, Souls can remain on Earth, remain under the Veil of Amnesia, but working for the betterment of the planet. I agreed this because these Ascended Masters (or 'junior Ascended

Masters' as we say when they are in the sixth dimension) have so much to teach the remaining Souls on the planet. And because of the level of their light vibrations, they raise the vibrations of the Earth.

Many people believed that 2012 would see the end of the world. This was a risk I am thankful you humans narrowly avoided through a collective outpouring of love and thanks during 2011. Particularly key was the 11th day of the 11th month of 2011, which we will discuss in more detail later in the Manual.

Not only did you manage to avoid annihilation of the planet, but you shifted the trajectory of the Earth. You have enabled the World to reach a higher 'potential' steady state. In simple words, it's more likely you'll achieve peace, prosperity and health for all, what we refer to as the Golden Age on Earth. The actions you take *now* will decide whether it is a rough or smooth transition. The balance of light now outshines the dark.

Continue shining this light. Augment it. Illuminate the world with your light, My beloved children who are reading this book, and you will bring about the Golden Age. It is why I have sent you this Manual. Because so much more needs to be done. Yet with your reading this Manual, the Golden Age will be achieved.

Tell others about the Manual, encourage them to read it – but don't push your enthusiasm onto others in a superior way. Everyone has personal choice and you cannot force belief on people. Allow them their free choice.

One last thing: by raising your own vibrations, you raise the vibrations of the world, so do not think you are powerless. Just one person reaching the seventh dimension can change the trajectory of the whole world. Make yourself count.

The Dimensions

Most people in the world exist in the third dimension. They are driven by greed, self-interest and fear. They live in conditions that reflect their mental state – either a fear of losing their immense wealth, position, influence and need to gain more, or a fear of not having enough money, love or security. Materialism abounds in the third dimension.

When the Soul progresses to the fourth dimension, that Soul has taken a step toward realising that materialism is not the be all and end all; they have taken a step toward spiritual development. They have also chosen to contribute in some way to the betterment of the planet or the people around them.

In the fifth dimension, this spiritual development is reinforced. The person decides very clearly that they want to work for the good of the planet in some way and, whilst fears and insecurities remain, they know there is more than being alone in the world. They know *something* is there, that God exists at some level.

By the sixth dimension you have reached the status of junior Ascended Master. You have a deep connection with Me, the Divine, and serve the planet and humanity on a larger scale. You still have lessons to learn. But once these have been largely learnt, in particular those of unconditional love and pure love for yourself and others, you can progress to the seventh dimension of fully Ascended Masters, the same dimension in which angels exist.

How Do You Raise Your Vibrations?

Chakras are energy centres in your bodies. It is imperative that you cleanse, heal and energise these chakras for full health, and to enable spiritual connection and Ascension. This chapter provides information on how to do this, as does Chapter 8.

In *The Lightseeker's Manual* I ask you to focus on the nine chakras in figure 1. Although there are many more chakras in your energy systems, working on these will enable you to Ascend. In ascending order from below the feet to above the head, these are the Earth star, base or root, sacral, solar plexus, heart, throat, third eye, crown, and star chakras.

For those who can see chakras, they look like small vortices emanating from the body. Because of the way the body's electromagnetic field is defined, chakras should twist clockwise to be smooth and healthy. Each chakra relates to a specific issue or emotion, such as love, power or creativity. If the person has a negative attitude to the particular issue or emotion, the chakra will spin anticlockwise.

Chakras can change direction during the course of the day if shaken by an event or experience. If there is no energy coming from the chakra, as the human is blocked by a particular emotion or issue, this can also have negative health consequences, as explained in greater detail in chapter 8.

Honour your chakras. Love them as you should love your bodies, for these energy doorways are your gateways to health and abundance.

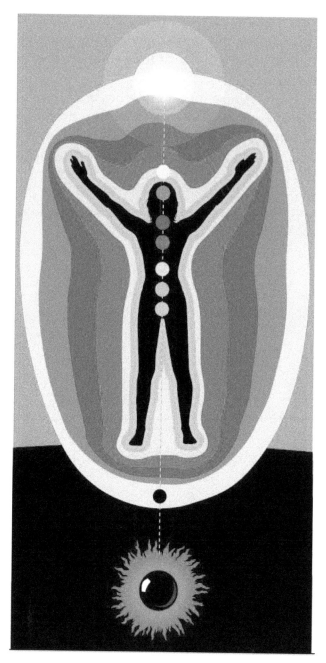

Figure 1: The Nine Priority Chakras for Ascension

The Earth Star Chakra

The Earth star chakra is about 30cm beneath the ground and resonates with black obsidian in all dimensions. It is guarded and guided by Archangel Sandolphon. This is your potential. If this chakra is not functioning properly, your potential will be limited – you could stagnate, not just spiritually but also in terms of your whole physical experience. It is essential to ignite the Earth star because without being grounded in the physical, you cannot manifest your hopes and dreams in everyday life. **The affirmation for this chakra is 'I AM One with the Earth'** – because, dear beloveds, you are intrinsically connected with the Earth. The 'I AM...' prefix represents your wish and commitment to resonate with your highest form, your blueprint. If you repeat, 'I AM One with the Earth,' you are recognising your intrinsic connection to the Earth.

The Veil of Amnesia has made you forget this, but understand the interconnectedness you have with everything on the planet, with every particle, the soil, the rocks, crystals, the mammals, the ocean, the air, every living creature. Know you are part of a field, an electromagnetic field that flows through everything.

The Base Chakra

Located at the base of the spine, the base chakra is guarded and guided by Archangel Gabriel. Whereas the Earth star chakra resonates with black obsidian, the base chakra moves from red (in the third dimension) to rose-gold (in the seventh).

This is the seat of your power, your instincts, your connectedness to survival. This is where the seat of your physical health and wellbeing lies. **In the seventh dimension the affirmation for this chakra is 'I AM the support of the world'. In the fourth and fifth dimension it is 'I AM supported'.**

This chakra tells you to remember you are all intrinsically supported because I, Source, God, support you all the time. Remember I support you *all* the time, and when you join me in the seventh dimension, you will be part of the support for the planet.

The Sacral Chakra

The sacral chakra is the home of sensuality and sexuality, the balance of male and female energies. It is also guarded and guided by Archangel Gabriel. Anticlockwise or blocked sacral chakras can lead to problems such as impotence and cancer. **The affirmation of this chakra in the seventh dimension is 'I co-create with the Universe'**, because in the seventh dimension you know you are one with Me and I create all things.

In the fourth and fifth dimensions the respective affirmations are 'I am flow' and 'I create my own reality'. The colour to resonate with in the seventh dimension is peach-gold and in the third, orange.

There is also the naval chakra in this area, but working with the sacral will be enough to enable your Ascension.

The Solar Plexus Chakra

Guarded and guided by Archangel Uriel, if this chakra is blocked or spins anticlockwise fear is the driving force of the individual. They may be subject to power games and aggressive behaviour.

In the seventh dimension this chakra resonates with the colour shimmering gold and in the third dimension, yellow. **In the seventh dimension the affirmation is 'I AM the power of the Universe'. In the third dimension it is 'I AM strength'.**

The Heart Chakra

In the seventh dimension this chakra is shimmering gold-pink; in the third dimension it is pink or green. **In the fourth and fifth dimensions the affirmation is 'I am unconditional love'. In the seventh dimension it is 'I AM pure love'.**

Guarded by Archangel Chamuel, this chakra is incredibly important. Blocked or anticlockwise heart chakras prevent people from being able to experience full loving relationships, be they with lovers, friends or with humanity.

The Throat Chakra

The throat chakra is guarded and guided by Archangel Michael. Pale blue in the third dimension, in the seventh dimension it is shimmering gold and royal blue. **In the seventh dimension the affirmations are 'I speak the truth' and 'I AM the Divine truth'.**

The Third Eye

In the middle of the forehead, the third eye chakra is guarded and guided by Archangel Raphael. In the third dimension, this chakra resonates with the colour indigo. In the seventh dimension, it resonates with golden lilac. **The affirmation in the seventh dimension is 'I know the Divine truth'.**

The Crown Chakra

About 10cm above the head, the crown chakra is guarded and guided by Archangel Jophiel. In the third dimension it resonates with violet. In the seventh dimension it resonates with gold-violet. **The affirmation in the seventh dimension is 'I draw in the knowledge of the world'.**

The Star Chakra

The last chakra you need to understand for your Ascension is the star chakra. This chakra is the gateway to Me, to Source, to God, to the Divine. By opening this chakra, you let in the flow of My Divine wisdom and love. By having your other chakras open and turning clockwise, you can draw in the Divine world through you to the Earth, *bringing Heaven down to Earth.*

The star chakra is guarded and guided by Archangel Metatron. It resonates with the colour crystal white in all dimensions. **The affirmation is 'I AM One with the Divine', for you are One with Me.**

Raising Your Vibrations to Move through the Dimensions

☼ Exercise 1: Select a Journal ☼

Select a beautiful or meaningful journal in which you can record your thoughts and take notes. *The Lightseeker's Manual* will take you on an exciting inner journey.

In your journal, record all the significant events currently happening in your life, as these may be lessons you need to learn in order to progress your Ascension quickly. Record what works for you and what you find difficult. Often what you find most difficult is an indication of the area in which you are most guarded.

☼ Exercise 2: Set Your Intention ☼

You are entering a new phase of your life. It is important that you recognise the significance of your decision to read this book and undertake the exercises within it. Your life will change from this point. You will begin to connect with your Guardian Angel and other celestial beings who bring My messages to you.

Start with a significant ritual. Look at your diary and see how you can make space for regular meditations and visualisations, or just say a special prayer of thanks to Me and the celestial world for standing with you.

You may wish to fast for the day, by avoiding meat, caffeine and alcohol. You do not need to avoid food completely, but mark this occasion in some way, as you are on the front step of the passageway to join Me.

☼ Exercise 3: Energise Your Chakras ☼

Practise imagining each chakra pulsing with the light with which it resonates in the seventh dimension. Start with the Earth star chakra and work up to the star. With each chakra, as well as imagining the beautiful pulsing colour, focus on the seventh-dimensional affirmation. Do this at least three times per week. Table 1 summarises the chakras, their colours and affirmations in the seventh dimension, along with the Archangel who works closely with the chakra.

Table 1 Chakra Characteristics in the Seventh Dimension

Chakra	Archangel	Colour the chakra resonates with in the 7th dimension	Affirmation(s) in 7th dimension
Earth	Sandolphon	Black obsidian	I AM One with the Earth
Base	Gabriel	Rose-gold	I AM the support of the world
Sacral	Gabriel	Peach-gold	I co-create with the Universe
Solar Plexus	Uriel	Shimmering gold	I AM the power of the Universe
Heart	Chamuel	Gold-pink	I AM pure love
Throat	Michael	Shimmering gold and royal blue	I speak the truth and I AM the Divine truth
Third eye	Raphael	Golden lilac	I know the Divine truth

Crown	Jophiel	Gold-violet	I draw in the knowledge of the world
Star	Metatron	Crystal white	I AM One with the Divine

☼ Exercise 4: Walk in Nature ☼

Being in nature allows us to disentangle human auras from each other. Cities and polluted places hold a lot of negative energy. Without realising it, people emit a concoction of toxic energy. If you do not protect yourself against this energy, it can drag down your vibrations. Nature does the reverse: it cleanses, uplifts and heals.

☼ Exercise 5: Eat Glorious and Healthy Food ☼

This does not mean starve yourself of goodies like chocolate or cakes, but recognise that home-cooked food made with love is more nutritious than mass-produced shop-bought food.

Ask your body what food it requires to be healthy. Your body holds all the answers. As humans, you have forgotten that each cell in your body is capable of individual thought and feeling.

Connect to each body part to ensure you maximise your physical health. You can also heal your food before eating. Stand it in the Golden Silver Violet flame of transmutation, which you will learn about later.

And do not use microwaves; or if you have to, minimise the use. This form of cooking kills the goodness in food and puts you in contact with harmful rays that reduce your vibrations. If used a lot, they can leave you with permanent auric damage.

☼ Exercise 6: Meditate ☼

Rather than visualisations (which this Manual focuses on), meditation is about relieving the mind of the need to think, process or do.

It allows the mind to be at peace. Breathing is a key part of this relaxation of the physical and mental body. If your breathing is relaxed, you send the message to the brain that there is no need to worry.

☼ Exercise 7: Live in Harmony with the Earth ☼

Many of you reading this Manual will be aware of the challenges you are creating for the Earth's health: pollution, extraction of resources – but most of all, *too much waste.*

There is plenty for all, but a few are taking more than their share. Know that there is an *abundance* of resources. This means there is *plenty for everyone.* Even so, take care of the environment around you and minimise your waste. What you can't *reduce,* recycle. In your hearts, you will know what needs to be done.

☼ Exercise 8: Enjoy Life ☼

Music, laughter and healthy dancing are all exquisite ways of raising your vibrations.

☼ Exercise 9: Physical Exercise ☼

Exercise in moderation, as this is essential to raise your vibrations.

Example Timetable for Weeks 1 and 2

This is only an example of the programme you may wish to keep. You should fit the course around your life. Meditations can be performed in the morning before you go to work, in the evening, or even last thing at night. However, visualisations are always best done sitting up. Otherwise, it is very easy to fall asleep and lose the full benefit of the visualisation.

Good luck.

Example Timetable Weeks 1 and 2

Activity	Week 1 by Day							Week 2 by Day						
Open your *Lightseeker's Manual* journal and start writing. (1)														
Set your intention and prepare your diary for the week. (2)														
Start your chakra visualisations. (3)														
Walk in nature or a park, or sit in a beautiful garden. (4)														
Reflect on your diet. How can you nurture yourself more? Begin integrating your new diet. (5a)														
Talk to your body. How does your body feel? Be more in touch with your body. (5b)														
Meditate. (6)														
Review how you are living in harmony with the planet. Are there improvements you can make? (7a) Make at least one change in the next 2 weeks. (7b)														
Have fun – music, dance, laughter. (8)														
Moderate exercise. (9)														

Chapter 2

CONNECTING WITH THE CELESTIAL WORLD

Angels are beings of love and light whose vibrations are so quick, they are invisible to the naked eye unless a person has advanced psychic abilities. Angels are My gift to you. It is one way the Divine celestial kingdom can be brought to Earth, for they are messengers of My word and My love and I have sent millions to you.

Angels vibrate at the same frequency as I, for they are part of Me. Whilst all are equal in the angel kingdom, some are more advanced than others.

Each one of you who incarnates on the planet Earth has your own Guardian Angel. This Guardian Angel is with you from your first incarnation on Earth throughout your lives on that planet. They are partners with you. They love you unconditionally and purely.

They are always there to help, but they cannot interfere unless you request them to do so, for all humans have free will. The only exception we make is if you are about to die when it is not yet your time. Then the angels are allowed to intervene to save your life.

Guardian Angels have a very special relationship with you because you share them with no other Soul. Therefore, I urge you to develop your relationship with your Guardian Angel, ask for their assistance, ask for their presence to be known to you. You may find you see signs of their presence, whether it's small white feathers or something you read, hear or see; voices in your head, knowledge that they are with you.

The more advanced angels are Archangels, who lead thousands of angels. Archangels and angels specialise in particular roles. It may be protection, it may be tranquillity, it may be healing.

There are angels of marriage, helping keep your marriages together. If you divorce, it is very important that you let those angels know you no longer wish for them to help you stay with that particular person. When you marry, you send out a signal to the Universe stating that you and your partner are now a single being. If you divorce, you must send out the same signal saying you are now separate. Divorce is a very significant vow, just as marriage is.

There are other types of angelic force that work closely with Me, such as seraphim and cherubim. They work at different levels and have different functions, vibrating in the seventh dimension or above and devoted to the best and highest path of the Universe. Many of these will be there at your call if you request them to work with you for the betterment of the planet. But it is Archangels and angels whom you most need to understand in the angelic kingdom.

There are four main ways of psychically connecting with celestial beings such as angels and Ascended Masters. These are:

Claircognizance – You ask a question of the angelic kingdom and the answer comes to you. Whether you call it 'gut instinct' or the answer is just there in your head, the answer comes and you know it to be the truth.

Clairvoyance – You may see the answer in pictures in your head, or you may see celestial beings around you with your naked eye. These may appear as shadows or as fully formed figures, depending upon your level of psychic connection.

Clairaudience – You hear the voices of celestial beings clearly in your head, or even outside in the room.

Clairsentience – You feel the Divine presence within your body or around you.

Whichever form of psychic gift you have, welcome it. It may be that one gift is stronger than others, but they can all be developed, and from 2012 psychic abilities will become much more commonplace. The strength of your psychic ability is not directly related to the dimension you have attained. I ask you to practise your connection with the celestial world, for by connecting with us, we can help you. Ask us, but always ask with gratitude.

Grounding

Grounding is essential for you to remain at your highest vibrations and in your best health. Grounding enables you to draw energy from the Divine kingdom into your everyday physical lives. It enables your dreams to become reality. It allows the etheric thought forms to present themselves in the physical world.

Do not think for one minute that I want you wandering around with your head in the clouds, daydreaming about connecting with Me. I want you solidly grounded in the physical, as this is where the most rapid improvement to the world will be achieved.

The world is not a mental construct; it is a physical sphere of experience. My challenge to you is to connect to Me and My celestial kingdom, and then bring the wisdom, abundance and joy we hold here to the Earth and your everyday lives.

How to Ground Yourself

You can imagine tiny roots growing from the soles of your feet, or be very aware of how the soles of your feet feel on the Earth. You can even imagine connecting to the Earth's centre.

I want you to *know* you are part of the Earth – not just connected but *part* of the electromagnetic field that flows through all living creatures in and on the planet.

Protection

Protection is also key. Protection is there for your asking. I have sent millions of angels to protect you from all negativity coming toward you. Protection is not just necessary if you are connecting to the celestial kingdom, but all the time, to maintain your vibrations. Without protection, your aura is open to interference from the auras of others around you who are stressed and anxious.

When you walk into a busy place like a shopping complex or a bustling city, do you feel more tired than when you walk in nature or contemplate a beautiful view? This is because in nature, the air cleanses and heals, but where there are toxins and pollution, the air is heavy and contaminated. These drag down your vibrations.

Protection is also necessary from any negativity that may come from within you. Thoughts need constant herding. Negative thoughts drag down the vibrations and have a rippling effect on all other aspects of life.

How to Protect Yourself

Archangel Michael is invaluable for protection. It is his special gift and he leads a legion of angels of protection. I have sent you Archangel Michael so that you need never be scared or anxious.

Each morning and evening, call on him to surround you with a ball of his protective blue energy. Alternatively, use the protection of pure love from the Christ Energy that Jesus carried to Earth.

(1) Example of Grounding and Protection

Feel your feet firmly on the floor. Breathe deeply and evenly, and feel yourself relaxing. With each intake of breath, inhale a beautiful white light of purification and protection. As you breathe out, this light releases all the tension from your body.

Breathe the white light into your feet and ankles; now breathe out the tension. Breathe the brilliant white light into your calves and knees, and breathe out the tension. Feel the white light filling your thighs, hips and buttocks; now breathe out the tension. The white light flows along your spine and internal organs, and as you breathe out, you release all the tension you've been holding there.

Breathe the white light into your arms, hands and fingers. As you breathe out, your body feels more and more relaxed and heavy. The white light now flows into your neck, face and head, your ears and eyes, and as you breathe out, it takes all the tension and worries of the day with it. This is the white light of purification, of relaxation, of protection.

In your feet, feel tiny golden roots growing down into the magical soil, bonding you with love to the energy of the Earth. Breathe in this magnificent energy that keeps you grounded and strong.

Continue to breathe deeply and evenly. Ask Archangel Michael to place his blue cloak of protection around your shoulders. Feel its weight on your shoulders. He zips it up beneath your feet and brings the hood over your upper chakras. Ask him to place an angel of protection before you, one behind you, one above you, one below you, one to the left of you and one to the right of you. You are now 100% protected.

The Mahatma Energy

The Mahatma Energy was brought to Earth by Mahatma Gandhi. Until now, it was the most powerful energy gifted to this planet to aid with Ascension. Alongside the Golden Silver Violet flame, these instruments are invaluable for raising your vibrations and releasing karma. They can increase the rate of your spiritual development a thousand fold. Mahatma Gandhi is now an Ascended Master and still works closely with this energy.

It is a loving, harmonious, peaceful energy, yet powerful and transformative. Its power is in the rate of acceleration it can bestow upon those who use it in good faith.

As long as you use it with the intention to serve your higher purpose and that of the world, it will lift your vibrations rapidly. However, woe to those who use it for their own end, as the converse of the Mahatma is that it accelerates the diminishing vibrations of a Soul.

Take heed, as it can also bring to the fore life challenges you have yet to face. But know that this is necessary, especially at this time.

How to Use this Energy

The Mahatma Energy can be used to reprogramme your DNA. It can therefore reduce or still your rate of aging. It can be used to overcome physical and auric diseases (physical disease always manifests first in the auric level).

It can also be used to reprogramme cells and to heal. It can be used on Earth to heal toxins in the planet created by man or other sources. It can be used to open portals or cleanse ley lines. It is mighty and it is My gift to the world.

To work, the Mahatma Energy must connect through a person to the Earth – it is a direct fast track energy highway for Divine energies to pour straight into Earth. The person is the essential interconnector.

Therefore, when using it, ask it to pass through your body and aura into the Earth. To set your intention for the Mahatma

Energy to be used for the good of the planet, in requests add, 'I commit myself in service to the Divine,' or, 'I ask for the Mahatma Energy to flow through my body and aura into the Earth to aid the best and highest path of the planet and Universe.' The Archangel who works closely with the Mahatma Energy is Archangel Metatron.

⦿Visualisation⦿
The Mahatma Energy

Feel beautiful strong roots growing from the soles of your feet deep down into Mother Earth, connecting with her centre.

Ask Archangel Michael to wrap you in his cloak of protection and post an angel before you, behind you, above you, below you, to the left and to the right of you.

Ask the mighty Archangel Metatron to guide you in this visualisation to bring down the Mahatma Energy, the most powerful energy gifted to this planet.

Ask the Archangel Metatron to bring the energy into your crown first, about 10cm above your head. Visualise this area being filled with an incredible golden platinum light that creates a wonderful sunshine feeling above your head. Feel it spinning in a clockwise direction. You can feel its power, you can feel its goodness, you can feel its healing, you can feel its love.

Now ask the Archangel Metatron to bring the Mahatma Energy through the crown of your head, into your third eye. Feel it expanding your third eye centre, allowing your psychic abilities to develop.

Feel the connection to the Divine kingdoms, to Source. Become aware of how you KNOW the Divine communication, how you FEEL the Divine communication, how you HEAR the Divine communication and how you SEE the Divine communication. Feel this golden platinum light spinning clockwise in your third eye centre.

Now ask the Archangel Metatron to bring the Mahatma Energy from your third eye to your throat. Feel it expand your ability to communicate the Divine messages. Feel it expand your wisdom, your goodness, your power to work for the Divine for the best and highest path of the planet. Feel this beautiful golden platinum light in your throat. Feel it spinning clockwise.

And now ask the Archangel Metatron to bring the Mahatma Energy into your heart centre, pulling it there, pulling it down from Source, through your crown, through your third eye, through your throat, into your heart chakra. Feel the energy expand in your heart chakra. Feel it increase the rate of your spiritual growth a thousand fold. Feel its love, unconditional and pure. Feel its power, working for the good of all. Your heart chakra is expanding and it feels good. Feel it spinning clockwise and radiating out from your heart centre, out into your aura, and into the air around you.

Feel yourself shining like a beacon of light in the world. Feel unconditional love for humanity, for the animal kingdom, for the planet, for the Universe. Know your connection to Source.

◎ Now ask the Archangel Metatron to pull the Mahatma Energy into your solar plexus. Feel the golden platinum energy expand in your solar plexus. Feel all fears leave you, replaced by fearlessness.

You now know your true potential and your true power to make a difference in the world. You are ready to stand in your full potential as a light-worker.

◎ Ask the Archangel Metatron to pull the Mahatma Energy into your sacral area. Feel the golden platinum energy heal this area in your abdomen. Know your ability to create.

Know your ability to heal – to heal the planet, to heal humanity's errors. Feel the Mahatma Energy spin clockwise in this area. Feel the golden platinum light expand out of your body, into your aura and beyond. Know you have the power to co-create with the Universe for goodness.

◎ Ask the Archangel Metatron to pull the Mahatma Energy into your base. Feel the golden platinum energy expand, healing this area. Feel the power of this energy. Feel its intensity, its reach, its beauty. Feel it spin clockwise. Know that you support the world.

Ask the Archangel Metatron to bring the Mahatma Energy into your Earth star chakra. This chakra is about 30cm below your feet, in the Earth.

The Earth star chakra is your potential. If you energise this chakra, you will reach your full potential.

By bringing the Mahatma Energy into the Earth star chakra, the Archangel Metatron is gifting you your full potential to be whatever you want to be on this Earth, and the full potential to be a light-worker. This can change the course of the planet and increase its trajectory so the Earth can Ascend.

Embrace the Mahatma Energy as part of your full potential. Feel the golden platinum energy spinning clockwise. Feel it connecting to the ley lines of the Earth until there are grids of golden platinum energy across the whole planet, with you at the centre.

Now ask Archangel Metatron to bring the Mahatma Energy from your Earth star chakra to the core of the Earth, the centre of Mother Earth.

Now ask Source to open your star chakra, the highest chakra in your aura, to let in the full flow of the Mahatma Energy direct from Source, through your aura and your body, through your Earth star and into the centre of the Earth.

Feel the golden platinum energy flowing through you, directly from God. It flows directly through you into the Earth, reaching out through the ley lines across the whole Earth's surface, until you and your aura are a ball of golden platinum light blazing in the Earth. The Earth becomes a blazing ball of golden platinum Mahatma Energy.

If you are ready to make your commitment to be a light-worker for the good of the Earth, make your commitment to Source and the Archangel Metatron now.

Source, the Archangel Metatron and the celestial world thank you for your commitment. And if you are not yet ready to commit, know that we love you unconditionally. If and when you are ready, we will be ready to work with you for the good of the planet. Know that your spiritual progress has already increased a thousand fold by bringing in the Mahatma Energy.

Become aware of your feet on the ground. Rub your thumbs with your fingers and roll your shoulders gently. When you are ready, open your eyes.

The Golden Silver Violet Flame

The Golden Silver Violet flame is one of My most treasured gifts to Earth. It has been carried to Earth by various Ascended Masters over the past hundred years. As I have trusted you more to use it wisely, so have I augmented the power of the flame.

First the violet, then the silver, and finally the gold have been brought. Now the flame is a powerful energy that transmutes all negativity and turns it to pure positivity.

The Ascended Master who works closely with the flame is St Germain, who also enjoyed an incarnation as Merlin. The Archangel guarding and guiding use of the flame is Archangel Zadkiel. Call on either Zadkiel or St Germain to aid your use of the flame.

It can be used multiple times throughout the day and night. In particular, it can be used to stop the accumulation of additional karma, as if you ask to stand within the Golden Silver Violet flame, all negative karma that you have created can be transmuted to pure positivity.

It can rid you of all negative karma, if the Lords of Karma agree that this be done. It can also stop the accumulation of new karma. However, do not think of using it for the ends of the Ego, to wield it with the intention of committing wrong after wrong and then transmuting those wrongs. It will only work if you use it for the benefit of the planet. And if I see its misuse is widespread, I will withdraw it.

It is also a powerful energy to use in daily and night-time protection. You can stand yourself in a pillar of the flame, and ask St Germain or Archangel Zadkiel to blaze a trail of the flame before you throughout your day, so negativity coming your way will be turned to pure positivity.

It can also be used to heal disagreements between people at work, home or around you. Stand the person with whom you would like to clear negativity in the flame and it will work its magic. This is My gift to you. Use it wisely.

◎ Visualisation ◎
Connecting with Your Guardian Angel

Find a quiet spot in your busy day and sit comfortably, your feet on the floor and arms unfolded. Your spine should be straight and your shoulders open. This is the ideal meditative position. Whilst lying on the floor is possible, it can result in sleep. Sitting in a chair or cross-legged on the floor works well.

Your breathing is very important. Calm your breathing, making it even and deep. Close your eyes and become conscious of the air flowing in and out of your body. Now ask to be taken to your spiritual home.

This is a place in your inner consciousness where you always love to go. If you have never experienced your inner home, ask to travel there now. It may be a small hut on a mountain, or a grand palace by a forest, or a glade where you can simply sit. Wherever you are transported, allow yourself to be taken.

You are now at your inner home. Look around you. Become conscious of the scenery, of the colours, of the texture of the ground beneath your feet. You feel deeply at home.

This is where you are in control; you can do anything in this inner realm. You can fly, swim underwater, run up trees, or simply be at peace sitting for hours. Explore this inner home, and when you are ready, come to rest. It is time for you to meet with your Guardian Angel.

Ask your Guardian Angel to appear in front of you. You feel a powerful, loving energy when they arrive. Enjoy the love your Guardian Angel is sending you, pure love for you.

Thank your Guardian Angel for the lifetimes you have spent learning and growing together. This is your time with your Guardian Angel. Ask their name and accept any name they give you. Ask any questions you may have. Take heed of any guidance your Guardian Angel may give you.

When you are ready, your Guardian Angel wraps their wings around you and you feel the protection of their love for you. They now give you a gift. Take this gift, for it is a symbol of an important lesson you have to master in this lifetime. If it makes no immediate sense, take it with you in your pocket and reflect on what it means later.

Know that you can always return to your inner home and be with your Guardian Angel whenever you wish. They are always with you everywhere, but can only assist you if you ask for help. It is easy to ask for help. Just think, say out loud or write down a request and listen to the answer in your dreams, in your heart, gut or head, or watch for signs they may send in your everyday life.

With My love, Source.

Spirit Guides

Angels are My messengers to you, but there are many other celestial beings who are keen to work with you in your personal development, such as spirit guides. Spirit guides are animals or humans who are willing to work with you for your own personal growth. Not all spirit guides are in the seventh dimension.

A deceased ancestor may be a very willing spirit guide, but take note: if you did not value the wisdom of a deceased relative when they were alive, do not take as rote what their spirits advise you. They will have additional knowledge and experiences, having entered the celestial kingdom, but they may not be able to give you the wise guidance of a being from the seventh dimension.

Animal spirits can make powerful guides and I encourage you to harness their strength and insight. By tapping into animal spirit guidance, you can master certain character traits that species of animals have mastered.

Do not make the mistake of thinking household pets or wild animals are uncivilised and less enlightened than you. Animals are powerful spiritual leaders who, like humans, are at various stages of development.

When seeking advice, I advise you to ask for guidance from animal spirits that have already reached the seventh dimension. If you want to enhance a particular characteristic within your own persona, such as strength, courage, wisdom, perseverance or insight, tapping into animal spirits in the seventh dimension can be a very powerful aide. Remember all are in My Kingdom and I have created all equal.

I hear you ask about eating meat. As you progress to the seventh dimension, you will find eating meat more and more difficult as you become increasingly aware of the God-spark within every living creature.

However, in the Earthly kingdom the physical body has certain needs and for these needs, meat can sometimes be important. I ask you always to bless your food, and bless the Soul of the animal that has passed over to make you healthy.

Treat animals with love and respect and, if possible and you are ready, reduce the intake of living creatures. Embrace the seventh dimension where meat will cease to be necessary for your nutrition. Under no circumstances should you believe you are better than the creatures you ingest.

❂ Visualisation ❂
Meeting Your Animal Spirit Guides

Sit comfortably with your feet flat on the ground. Become aware of your breathing. Ask Archangel Michael to protect you in a blue ball of his light.

You find yourself in a meadow. Flowers and freshly cut grass make the air fresh and energised. Ask for your animal spirit guide to appear before you. In front of you may appear one, two, three or more guides.

Ask if they are from the seventh dimension or higher. If they are not, listen to what they have to say and decide whether you wish to work with them.

If they are in the seventh dimension or above, accept their words with thanks. Whatever animal has come to you, accept them without judgment. Ask each animal what lesson they have to teach you.

Thank them for their support and know you can call on them in any place, at any time.

Discuss a way with them that they can signal they are there when they need to tell you something. It may be a feeling you get, or a noise in your ear. They will find a way to signal that you need to connect to them.

Example Timetable for Weeks 3 and 4

Activity	Week 3 by Day							Week 4 by Day						
Commence grounding and protection upon waking and before sleeping.														
Undertake visualisation to bring through the Mahatma Energy.														
Practise using the Golden Silver Violet flame multiple times a day.														
Undertake the visualisation to meet your Guardian Angel.														
Make asking your Guardian Angel for advice part of your everyday practice.														
Undertake the visualisation to connect with your animal guides – draw on them regularly for the characteristics they can enhance.														
Continue to introduce changes to your diet and lifestyle, so you nurture yourself and live in harmony with the Earth.														

Chapter 3

UNCONDITIONAL LOVE AND THE EGO

'Unconditional love is happiness' is the most important law in the Universe. If you as humans loved each human and each creature on the planet *unconditionally*, there would be no war, no famine, no suffering because what you have you would share, what you know you would share. You would recognise the truth that each living creature is but another manifestation of Me, and thus another manifestation of you.

Unconditional love is the centre of all happiness and contentedness. If you feel restless, unloved or without purpose, it is because you do not love yourself unconditionally and therefore you do not love others unconditionally.

When we love someone unconditionally, we do not require them to love us back or respond in a certain way. If you find yourself withholding affection because your partner hasn't behaved the way you would like, or even using your affection as a bartering tool in a relationship with a friend, colleague or lover, you are placing conditions on your love.

Loving unconditionally also means you love a person whatever their imperfections. To love unconditionally, you take the step forward along your spiritual path and recognise the Divine in everyone. You look for and see the 'God-spark' that is within you all. You recognise the fundamental truth that you are all connected to Me, God, Source, and that there is a pure part of you – the essence of all that is good about you – that is intrinsically lovable.

The Heart Chakra

The heart chakra reflects the emotional state and development of the person, relating to issues of the heart, and love. If a person is closed to love, the heart chakra will be low on energy, or emit no energy. If the person has negative associations with love, be it friendly love or love of a sexual nature, the heart chakra will spin anticlockwise.

The state of a chakra is not constant; sometimes it may spin clockwise and at other times anticlockwise, reflecting the state of the person at that time. The aim is to work through all issues of the heart, to love purely and unconditionally, and then the heart chakra will be fairly constant in its energy levels and spin clockwise. This chapter will help strengthen the energy from your heart chakra and enable you to move through the dimensions, dealing with issues that pertain to love.

So how does unconditional love manifest in the everyday? Well, we discussed how you have different issues as humans, as you pass through the Earthly dimensions. In the third dimension, humans are driven by greed, by fear of not having enough; or if you have *too much,* driven by a fear of losing it.

People feel disconnected from others in the third dimension, even from close family members. **The heart affirmations in this dimension that are needed to reprogramme yourselves are 'I AM Connected' and 'I AM Touch'.** The colour of the heart chakra resonates with green.

As you move into the fourth dimension and take that first step along your spiritual path, reaching out and actively seeking more from life than physical gratification, the issues pertaining to the heart chakra develop into recognition of the humanity in all things.

Yet in this dimension people still fear opening themselves to pure love, and are very negative about themselves, their imperfections and weaknesses. In this fourth dimension people cannot comprehend that I, Source, have made them flawed in order to evolve. **In this dimension the affirmations are 'I AM One with Others' and 'I AM Feelings'.**

In the fifth dimension, humans need to master unconditional love. This does not mean you have to like everyone. In a busy office you may have colleagues you esteem, who make you laugh and you like being with. There may be others you severely dislike. But to operate in the fifth dimension and love each of these people unconditionally, you must respect the intrinsic God-spark within them.

Even if it is buried deeply, you must seek out the God-spark and find something to value in them. **The affirmation of the heart chakra in the fifth dimension is 'I AM Unconditional Love'.**

But the lessons do not stop here. For the pursuit of Ascension and enlightenment, you need to pass from the fifth dimension to the sixth. In this dimension you continue to see the beauty in all humans and creatures of the planet, whatever form they take. You recognise that even with mass murderers or rapists, it is not your right to judge at a Soul level.

Yes, you must have an Earthly retribution system, but at a Soul level, you must not believe you are better or worse than such criminals, for you do not know what is in their Soul contracts to make them commit these indecencies. Only I, and the celestial kingdom, know what motivates them.

It may be that they are placed on the planet to teach others specific lessons to fulfil their Soul contracts. It may be that they have seriously wronged Me. But in the sixth dimension, you recognise it is not for you to judge and be *superior*; it is for Me and My Karmic Panel to rule them in our own way, standing in the light of pure love. **In the sixth dimension the affirmations are 'I AM All Love' and 'I AM the Heart of the Universe'.**

In the seventh dimension, you join us in the celestial kingdom. You join the ranks of Ascended Masters. If you remain on Earth, the Veil of Amnesia thins. You consciously know your connection to all living things. You know that I flow through everything – every human, every animal, fish, plant, rock. You become like Me and My angels, My Ascended Masters and other beings on the celestial plane. You become **pure love**, all-loving, all–forgiving, whatever the misdemeanour. **The affirmation in the seventh dimension is 'I AM Pure Love'.**

Soul Contracts and Karma

You might not believe Earth is one of the most sought after training grounds in the Universe, but it is – because on Earth you are challenged by lessons that cannot be experienced anywhere else in the Universe.

That is why I place you on the planet, so you can explore and learn, and grow and improve, and become more powerful. Eventually you learn how to stand in your full power, which makes *Me* more knowing, more powerful, *more.*

Before you enter your first incarnation on Earth, a blueprint for your Soul is agreed with Archangel Gabriel and your Soul's Guardian Angel. The blueprint states the ultimate potential of the Soul and the key lessons that need to be mastered before Ascension can take place. Ascension is where the sixth dimension is attained and the Soul can graduate from the school of Earth, stop reincarnating, and continue learning in the celestial realms or other training grounds. Once on Earth, Souls reincarnate again and again until the lessons are completed.

When a person dies, their Soul must stand before the Karmic Board, a committee of Ascended Masters and cosmic beings, currently mostly female, called the Lords of Karma. Here the Soul will be assessed; their karma will be weighed up (good deeds against the bad) and recorded in the Akashic Records.

This is where the idea of Judgment Day came from. However, the assessment is done within the context of pure love and without judgment. The next step is for the Soul, their Guardian Angel and the Karmic Board to decide the key lessons for the next incarnation and identify the Soul contracts that need to be made.

Soul contracts are just that: contracts between Souls. One Soul may need to learn the lesson that they are lovable, and so a contract is made with another Soul who will reject them in their life to enable them to overcome this and understand their lovability.

A Soul may need to learn the lesson that they will always be supported, financially and otherwise. This Soul may then be born into a family who struggles to make ends meet.

Soul contracts can also have their roots in the need to repay karma. If in one lifetime you murdered your father, at a Soul level you may agree to repay that karma by being rejected by your father in a future birth. You may have been saved by a Soul in one lifetime and, in another lifetime, agree to return the good deed by contracting with that Soul.

Frequently you will have Soul contracts with the same Soul in different incarnations. You will learn together through multiple incarnations. Sometimes family members choose to reincarnate together, although not necessarily in the same family positions.

By understanding these Soul contracts and the workings of karma, you will learn to recognise your most challenging relationships as enabling you to progress along your best and highest path. It is important to understand the patterns in these relationships, the defining emotions and challenges, for these people are there to help you learn your lessons; if you ignore the lessons, you will face the same lessons and challenges in other incarnations.

The people you find most difficult or have hurt you the most become your *best teachers*. In this way, you can honour them at a Soul level with unconditional love, and release hurt and resentment. Lessons of the heart revolve around knowing you are intrinsically 'lovable' and part of the infinite flow of love in the Universe.

Unconditional Love and Forgiveness

Unconditional love and forgiveness are very closely linked. If you love unconditionally, seeing past people's exterior imperfections to their Soul, forgiveness will flow.

A Soul contract is a deep and powerful connection. You will most definitely have Soul contracts with your parents, in the significant sexual relationships in your life, with your husband, wife or partner, with your close friends, with your children. The main relationships in your life are not formed by chance. They are designed this way so in each lifetime, you have the maximum chance to grow and progress toward Ascension.

Earth is a wonderful arena for learning, where you have free will once on the planet and free will in the celestial kingdom to choose your next lifetime's lessons. I urge you to use your time on Earth well, for if you don't, you will have to learn the lessons again and again and again in future lifetimes, and not necessarily on Earth.

Finally, it is an incredibly important time in the world's evolution. This generation will not be incarnating again on this planet in its current form, so make this lifetime matter.

Unconditional Love and the Self

Why do you not love yourselves? Know that I, Source, God, Allah have placed you in this Earthly kingdom in an imperfect form on purpose. Where would the lesson be if you were without challenges? It would not provide you with the tools to learn or grow.

It is not that I want you to suffer. You must learn you don't need to suffer, but true understanding will only come when you reconnect to Me in the seventh dimension. Until then, there are many lessons of the heart, the body and Soul.

Unconditional love for others starts with love of yourself. Are you hard on yourself? Do you constantly nag yourself, or chastise, or criticise what you have done? When you have made achievements, or just survived, do you congratulate yourself? Or do you keep going, thinking negative thoughts about how you should do better than this person or that person?

Are you constantly comparing yourself to other people who have more wealth, more love, more opportunities, more, more, more? Well, *stop*. You are needlessly making yourself suffer, and most likely those around you. You are also inhibiting your full enjoyment of all the things you desire in life because of the negative thoughts you are giving free reign.

If you are living in a toxic relationship, look inside you at the way you think about yourself. Do you love yourself dearly? Do you nurture the small child within you? Do you beam yourself love energy as you would beam love to Me or to a treasured family member? When you learn to love yourself, people around you will become more loving, or they will move out of your life to be replaced by people who love you unconditionally.

If you love yourself, the world around you will love you. This is a truth that you must own.

As an exercise, write down ten things you like about yourself. Now write down three things you love about yourself. If you can't think of any, look at yourself in a different way. Look at yourself through MY EYES. Can you see the love now? Can you feel the love for yourself? Love and forgiveness are very closely entwined, like a tight vine. Do you forgive yourself for the wrongs you have done in your life? Do you forgive yourself for being imperfect? Without learning to forgive yourself, you cannot love yourself unconditionally. Without forgiving others, you cannot love them unconditionally.

Whatever you have done in this life or in previous lives, if you truly repent, we will forgive you. If you choose to serve your best and highest purpose, and the best and highest purpose of the planet, we will forgive you. But we see into your heart; there are no secrets before the Lords of Karma. They assess your good and bad deeds in the light of pure unconditional love and if you do not repent in your heart, we will take necessary action.

I ask you to love yourselves unconditionally, just as we in the celestial kingdoms love you unconditionally. You are beautiful.

You are made in the perfect way to allow you to maximise your growth in each lifetime. Each day, you are able to start afresh and be the person you truly wish to be, standing in your full light on your best and highest path.

Know that the answer is within. Do not look for proof of lovability around you. Love yourself unconditionally and you will find an endless affirmation of your lovability around you.

Repetition

Repeat this Forgiveness Creed every day for thirty days and you will see improvement in the texture and quality of your life and yourself; for by repeating things regularly, you imprint them on your mind and body.

By repeating negative thoughts about yourself, they too are imprinted. Since birth, those around you – perhaps even your parents – have repeated negative statements to or about you. You must undo these negatives and replace them with positives. Throughout this book, use repetition as your friend. Think of repetition as reprogramming your mind, body and aura. Therefore, the more you repeat *I AM* mantras and positive affirmations, the more quickly changes in your life will occur.

Forgiving yourselves and others enables a huge leap toward Ascension. The Forgiveness Creed below is a simple statement of your intent to forgive yourself and others, and to embrace unconditional love.

Forgiveness Creed

I forgive all others for any harm they've done to me in this life, or previous lives, in this world, the Universe or any dimension.

I forgive myself for any harm I've done to another person, animal or thing in this life, or previous lives, in this world, the Universe or any dimension.

I forgive myself for any harm I've done to myself, and for all my imperfections, in this life and previous lives, in this world, the Universe or any dimension.

I choose to be a being of unconditional love and light, and to love myself unconditionally,

By seeking to be on my best and highest path, I am serving the world.

Etheric Retreats

Do not limit your minds by thinking growth and learning only happen when you are awake, or when you are confined within your physical body. The world is an amazing place. You are beings of physical and spiritual form. The spiritual form is an energy field that can defy the laws of gravity. It can leave your physical form and go exploring at night or when you sleep.

Always use your grounding and protection before you sleep to protect your Soul or light-body on these adventures. One very fast way to spiritual growth is to attend the etheric retreats of My particularly advanced celestial beings. These can be found in the ethers of the world – the world's aura. There are many retreats. Here I will highlight those retreats that are relevant for developing your heart chakra and your capacity for unconditional love.

Table 2 Celestial Beings for the Heart Chakra

Celestial Being	Quality	Etheric Retreat
Archangel Chamuel	Pure love	Mt Sinai
Archangel Zadkiel	Golden Silver Violet flame, transmuting all negativity to pure positivity Forgiveness	Temple of Purification over the islands of Cuba
Jesus	Pure love and the Christ Consciousness Energy of pure love	Temple of Resurrection, Jerusalem
Archangel Michael	Cutting the negative ties of the heart	Etheric retreat in Banff and Lake Louise, Canada
Archangel Sandolphon	Love of the Earth and your position in it	Jordan

Exercises for Unconditional Love

The following exercises are My recommendation to you to experiment with. Have fun, enjoy and stretch yourselves with each of these.

1) *Every day, look in the mirror and say, 'Hello, Amazing Being.'* Many humans find it difficult to recognise the God-spark in them, the part of Me that all humans possess. By repeating this daily greeting, you are reprogramming yourself to see your internal beauty and connection to Me.

2) *Forgive yourself your imperfections* by recognising you are given the perfect form for learning your lessons. How do you do this? If you find yourself being hard on yourself, consciously affirm your own worth and lovability. This doesn't mean you stop striving to improve and better yourself, but do it with love and tenderness. When you feel yourself becoming self-critical, replace this with a positive affirmation. For instance, if you start to think, 'I am so stupid. How could I have done that?' replace it immediately with, 'I forgive myself and recognise my Divine lovability. I am constantly improving.' Constantly herd your thoughts in this way.

3) *Radiate love to yourself* – sit quietly and imagine the feeling you get when you are falling in love, and radiate that energy to your own heart.

4) *Visualise your inner child* – your inner child is the part of you that is innocent and vulnerable. Your time as a child on Earth remains inside you. Hurts that were done to you as a child live within you unless you address them. It can help your Ascension greatly to work on healing this part of you. Hold, love and protect that child, and reassure them of their lovability.

5) *Repeat the Forgiveness Creed* presented in this chapter regularly, or for at least 30 days.

6) *Draw on the powers of My celestial beings* to heal your heart and increase the power of your love to help heal the world. Ask to work with Archangel Chamuel, who guards the heart chakra and leads the angels of love; Archangel Zadkiel, who commands the Golden Silver Violet flame; the angels of forgiveness; and of course your own Guardian Angel. To do this, simply quiet

your mind and ask the relevant celestial being to work with you on the goal you define. For instance: 'Dear Archangel Chamuel, please heal and strengthen my heart so my love enriches my own life and that of those around me.' Listen to any messages they may send to you. Record these messages in your journal.

7) *On different nights, visit the etheric retreats* of Archangels Chamuel, Michael, Sandolphon and Zadkiel and the Ascended Master Jesus. Before you go to sleep, ask your chosen celestial being to take you to their retreat. For instance: 'If it is in my highest path, please take me to the celestial retreat of Jesus.' Record any dreams or memories in your journal, but do not be surprised if you do not remember. You will still reap the benefits.

8) *Repeat the 'I AM' mantras* 'I AM pure love' and 'I AM the Golden Silver Violet flame'. Do this anytime, day or night, ideally out loud. This will set your intention for your energies to be aligned with this higher energy or purpose, and give us the go ahead to rain energy and blessings on you. Remember we cannot intervene unless you ask us.

9) *Laugh, have innocent / joyful fun,* nurture yourselves, honour yourselves. Do not be a martyr. Do something for yourself that makes you feel special.

10) *Enjoy yoga, ka huna dancing and body integration* or other energy enhancing exercise and healing therapies. Remember it is not just your physical body that needs nurturing. Your energetic body requires the healing and nurturing touch, too.

11) *Make your own massage oil* with base oil and rose essential oil and ask the angels to bless it. Then massage it into your heart chakra, in the centre of your chest.

The Christ Consciousness Energy

Jesus is one of My beloved Ascended Masters. He came to Earth with a specific mission: to bring the Christ Consciousness Energy to the planet and to you all. This energy is one of the most powerful energies in the Universe. It is the energy of pure love. This is why Jesus is such a role model for pure and unconditional love. I chose him because of his innate goodness. He came to Earth already an Ascended Master, yet with the Veil of Amnesia.

In 2012 a number of great cosmic portals were opened in the Earth, by this Channel and other light-workers in the world. You must cleanse, energise and protect these portals, for through their opening, they will allow in an abundance of the Christ Consciousness Energy that will heal the planet.

Ask for the Christ Consciousness Energy to flow through these great portals. You humans have free will and the more of you who ask, the more energy we will reign down upon you.

To carry the Christ Consciousness Energy yourself, you must be in the seventh dimension, e.g. a being of pure love. However, asking for the energy to fill you and surround you will help raise your vibrations to the seventh dimension.

You can ask Jesus and his twin flame Mary Magdalene to work with you on opening your heart chakra and becoming pure love.

The Ego

Beware of the Ego. The Ego is your conscious mind and is driven by fears and lack of comprehension that you are One with the Divine, with Me. It is the obstacle you need to overcome, having accepted the Veil of Amnesia upon incarnating on Earth.

Your Ego will chide you for not having the best job / house / income / beauty. When you become aware of a voice in your head chiding you, you become aware of the truth that your essence, your 'I AM', is separate from the Ego. This awareness is very powerful because then you can start turning the negative chides of the Ego to positive affirmations of who you are and what you can become.

The Ego might say, 'You'll never be successful with that shop. You're too disorganised, stupid, unlucky, unsupported....' The 'I AM' can then step in and counter, 'I run a successful shop because I'm wise, supported and organised.' In this way, you can manifest abundance in your life.

Be aware of why you want something. Do you want a promotion because it will make you feel you are as good as or better than those around you? Or do you want a new house because it will affirm that you are doing well in life? 'Things' feed the Ego's need to feel superior and the Ego's fears of not being worthy, loved or good enough.

Be aware of criticising, being angry and judging others, things and situations; of slating politicians, people and even whole cultures / races. By slating others, you put them down and feed your Ego's need to feel superior.

Collective Ego is one of the most destructive forces on the planet. Whole groups of people – sometimes whole nations – justify extreme behaviour because of the supposed wrongness of others and the rightness of their own views.

Religious wars and national conflicts have been built on this type of superiority. Force is sometimes necessary to protect oneself, but you should still try to approach it from a position of unconditional love. Look for possible evidence in yourself of behaviours that are demonstrated in your opponents, because often they are mirrors to your own inner world.

If you change your perspective on a person, they may well change their view of you, because with a change in your perspective, there is an energetic change that they will subconsciously pick up.

Do not think that if you say sweet things to your partner / boss but behind their back or subconsciously denigrate them, they won't pick it up. They will feel it subconsciously and respond. Every thought you have will have a reaction – unless you call in the Golden Silver Violet flame with the underlying goal of unconditional love.

Becoming Aware

The exercises in this next section are about becoming aware of the effect your thoughts and deeds have on others. Awareness is the first step to changing your behaviour. Do not be hard on yourself if you are not behaving in a fully loving way. Be proud of yourself for beginning to be conscious of how you relate to others. This is the first step toward unconditional love.

Gratitude is also an essential part of unconditional love. By showing gratitude, you are recognising the light in your life, and this awareness attracts more light. My celestial beings and I adore being thanked. The energy of gratitude is pure, not selfish. If it were given a colour, it would be a deep orange-gold. We bask in your gratitude energy. When you thank us for the bounty you have, we then want to give you more, so we can bask more in your gratitude. Gratitude is also part of understanding the bounty is not finite but a flow.

But remember to desire things for the intrinsic joy they give you and not to feed the Ego. It is also not about needing to be surrounded by an abundance of material things. These do not bring happiness. Love ultimately brings happiness, and bounty is about nature's beauty, prosperity in all its forms.

Awareness Exercises

1) Become conscious of how you feel this month on a physical and energetic level. Are you highly energised, or feeling low? Do you make others energised – at work, home, out shopping – or do you drain them of their energy? Do you smile, or are you grumpy? Do you assas-

sinate what people are wearing, what they look like or what they are doing, consciously or subconsciously?

2) In your journal, record your thoughts and experiences. Every day, find three things you are grateful for – different things each day. It could be a small thing: 'Thank you for enabling me to find a parking space easily.' Or a big thing: 'Thank you for my new promotion' or 'Thank you for the birth of my new niece.'

3) In your journal, capture any dreams or daydreams you may have. Often when you awake in the early hours of the morning you can remember your dreams, but if you don't write them down, by morning they are forgotten. We often send you messages in your dreams, though not always. Sometimes dreams are mere fragments of the day, or Ego-driven. But do pay attention. Write down your dreams and see if there are any patterns or insights you can glean in response to questions you have asked us. If you have a particular question you want answered, write it down before you go to sleep, address it to your Guardian Angel, or to one of My Ascended Masters or Archangels, and see what comes through in your dreams or daydreams.

Example Timetable for Weeks 5 and 6

Activity	Week 5							Week 6						
	1	2	3	4	5	6	7	1	2	3	4	5	6	7
Continue grounding and protection every morning upon waking, and every night before sleeping.														
Continue to modify your diet and lifestyle (to live harmoniously with nature), and connect with your Guardian Angel.														
Visualise bringing in the Mahatma Energy.														
Every day, greet your reflection in the mirror saying, 'Good morning, Amazing Being.'														
Radiate love to yourself. Know you don't have to be in a relationship to experience love – love starts with loving yourself.														
Herd your thoughts, replacing negative thoughts with positive.														
Visit Archangel Chamuel's etheric retreat at night for healing.														

Begin repeating the Forgiveness Creed – at least every 3 days for 30 days.														
Give thanks – every night find 3 things to be thankful for and write them in your journal.														
Ask to be filled with the Christ Consciousness Energy.														
Use your journal to capture your dreams, angel signs, thoughts, wishes and thanks.														

Chapter 4

MESSAGES FROM THE ASCENDED MASTERS

Ascended Masters are the most glorious, good, kind and wise women and men who have walked the planet. These are humans who have dedicated their lives to the betterment of the planet Earth, over the history of humankind. They sit with Me in the celestial world. Each has their specific quality or ability on which they can work with you if you have committed to improving yourself, or if you have committed to helping the planet Ascend.

Ascended Masters are celestial beings who exist in the seventh dimension, though they are not angels. They have followed a human evolutionary path. They are wise and loving, and work closely with Me for the betterment of the planet. However, unlike angels, they remain with some Ego and they retain free will.

Previously, a human had to reach the seventh dimension to become an Ascended Master. At that point, their Soul would Ascend and continue training in the celestial realms. With the efforts I, Source, God, Allah and the celestial world are focusing on Earth, we have granted a dispensation and to Ascend, you only need to reach the status of a junior Ascended Master in the sixth dimension.

Ascended Masters sometimes choose to return to Earth and incarnate once more to serve the best and highest path of the planet. There are only a handful of seventh dimension Ascended Masters walking the planet at present and most are unlikely to be aware of their status; as with all Souls, they have accepted the Veil of Amnesia. There are thousands of Ascended Masters in the celestial realms, many of whom you will have heard.

Ascended Masters sometimes work on a specific aspect of spiritual leadership. Jesus and Mother Mary both carry the Christ Consciousness Energy of pure love. St Germain, who was Merlin in an earlier incarnation, works with the Golden Silver Violet flame. Ray o' Light carries the Flame of Fearlessness.

Nelson Mandela is the most recently Ascended Master. He was placed on the Earth to promote the cause of justice, peace and forgiveness. Ask him to work with you on forgiveness and leadership qualities. He has now commenced his work from the other side in support of Africa's Ascension and that of the world.

Masters are particularly keen to work with you if you are committed to helping the planet or its people in some way. Connecting to a specific Master can help raise your vibrations.

If there is a particular quality you are looking to develop, connecting to the Master who resonates strongly with that quality can help you. If you have committed your life to the world in some way, there is likely to be a Master who wishes to work with you for all of your life. This Master is called your Over-Lighting Master, and it can be a very enriching, deep relationship.

The Masters mentioned below are particularly relevant for high-speed Ascension, although any Master will be enlightened and can aid you in your Ascension.

Each Master has an etheric retreat in the aura of the Earth, above the physical plane. You can ask to be taken to these etheric retreats either consciously with your light-body – the energetic part of you rather than the physical body – or unconsciously when you are asleep.

Schools and spiritual classes are conducted in the etheric retreats, as well as healing, cleansing and energising. Attending etheric retreats can swiftly increase your vibrations and the speed of your spiritual journey. You can visit a different etheric retreat each night, or the same one for many nights. You may receive a message to visit a particular retreat.

Otherwise, choose a retreat with a Master with whom you resonate, or with an issue you want to deal with or quality you wish to attract. For instance, if you find your life challenging and fear the future, visit Ray o' Light's etheric retreat above the Atlantic Ocean, off the coast of West Africa.

Table 3 Ascended Masters, Qualities and Retreats

Ascended Master	Quality	Etheric Retreat
Prophet Mohammed	Wisdom	Above Mecca, Saudi Arabia
Jesus, and Mother Mary	Unconditional love	Temple of Resurrection over the city of Jerusalem
Ray o' Light	Fearlessness	Off the coast of West Africa, in the Atlantic Ocean
St Germain	Manifestation	Macchu Picchu, Peru
Buddha	Transcending all Earthly concerns, and completely aligning with your highest Self (your highest potential)	Shamballa, Gobi Desert
Gandhi	Peace	Above Varanasi, India
Djwal Kul	Honour	Tibet

Florence Nightingale	Perseverance	Above the City in London
Serapis Bey	Direction and decision-making	Ascension Temple and Retreat at Luxor above the Luxor Temple
Isis	Humble beauty	Above the Giza Pyramid, Cairo, Egypt
Afra	Forgiveness	Above Table Mountain, Cape Town, South Africa
Lord Himalaya	Ascension through peace and silence, through the knowledge that all power is within, and a single drop of rain contains the truth of the world	Himalaya Mountains
Thor	Courage	Greece
Zeus	Power for the good of humanity	Turkey
Tabor	Truth, justice and honour	Mountains above Colorado Springs, USA
Goddess of Liberty	Freedom from oppression; emancipation and hope	New York
Nelson Mandela	Justice, peace, forgiveness	No retreat as yet

☼ Exercise ☼
To Take on the Quality of an Ascended Master

By repeating Alleluia Isis, Alleluia Serapis Bey or Alleluia Liberty again and again ('Alleluia Isis, Alleluia Isis, Alleluia Isis, Alleluia Isis'), you are aligning your 'I AM' with that particular Ascended Master and qualities they possess.

For instance, if you want to enhance your inner peace, repeat, 'Alleluia Gandhi, Alleluia Gandhi, Alleluia Gandhi.'

If you want to enhance your fearlessness, repeat, 'Alleluia Ray o' Light, Alleluia Ray o' Light, Alleluia Ray o' Light.' The more you repeat this mantra, the more you will resonate with the vibrations of the Ascended Master with whom you choose to identify. You may repeat this mantra with as many Ascended Masters as you choose.

☼ Exercise ☼
To Connect to a Master

If you wish to connect to a particular Master, simply relax into deep meditation, ground and protect yourself, and ask for that particular Master to work with you on the issue you have in mind. Listen to the messages from the Master. They may come to you in dreams, thoughts, words or sensations.

◎ Visualisation◎
To Find Your Over-Lighting Master

Breathe deeply. Feel tiny golden roots grow out of the soles of your feet, connecting you to the magical Earth. They extend deeper and deeper into the Earth's soil with each inhalation and exhalation. At the centre, they find a black obsidian crystal. The roots wrap themselves around that crystal, drawing in the Earth's powerful energy.

With each inward breath, bring that energy up through the roots and into your body. Ask Archangel Michael to enclose you in a bubble of his beautiful blue energy, protecting you completely.

Ask Archangel Gabriel to pour her crystal white energy of purification through your body and aura, leaving you completely cleansed.

You find yourself in a meadow. A small stream meanders beside you and flowers dot the grass. You feel warm sun on your bare arms and birds sing as they go about their daily chores. The scent of summer is in the air.

In the distance, you see a figure walking toward you. The figure rapidly approaches and before you see their face, you feel their immense power and love for you and for the world. This is your Over-Lighting Master. It may be a man or a woman. Feel honoured to have this Master work with you in your life.

The Master greets you. Ask them their name, and what specific qualities or aims they want to work with you on.

Ask you Master any questions you have; listen to their answers and any guidance they have to give you.

Thank your Over-Lighting Master. When you are ready, become aware of your feet on the ground, rub your fingers and thumbs together, and open your eyes.

There now follow a number of messages channelled from the Ascended Masters. They have been specifically given for this Manual.

Message from Gandhi

It is I, Gandhi. It is a pleasure to be with you and to be able to communicate this message for the Manual. We are all aware of it and excited by the implications this Manual has for the planet and its Ascension. This is my message to the world.

It was not easy to tread the path I took, one of no resistance, but of peace. But as you have seen, peace is the greatest power. It is the power of Light. And when faced with this Light, all darkness melts away.

It is not conquered overnight, but with the knowledge of the God we follow in our hearts. We know we shall always be victorious when the cause is just. I ask that you look inside and find the courage – the courage to stand up for what you know is right.

What is right is that people should live in harmony, free to carry out their daily lives without the fear of harm coming to them. We know that women and those weaker need protecting and not violating. And women, **know** that you must also stand up – know your truest worth and power, for without self–knowledge, you will allow others to exploit you.

There is much that you know is right and yet you do not follow. The constant use of resources and waste is not necessary to live a wealthy life. It is not enough to recycle; you must invest in products that do not create waste in the first place, such as papers and wholly recyclable materials. Where possible, cut out the packaging completely.

You wonder why I, an Ascended Master, am concerned about the state of the environment. But everyone up here is concerned about the peril you are putting the beautiful world in. When an island of plastic is created in the Pacific, one of the last pristine environments of the world, something must change. And the only ones who can change it are you.

I have not mentioned love, but you must carry love in your hearts – love for yourself, forgiveness for yourselves, but also love and forgiveness for those around you. Only God has the right to judge, and you do not know the Soul contracts people have made, the lessons they have agreed to learn in this world. Only the celestial realm knows that. So do not judge; do not hate, but love; find your strength in peace and in resistance of what you know to be unjust.

That is my message. I am here to work with you, always. With my love, Gandhi.

Message from Jesus

Here is my message for the Manual.

Children of God, you are the chosen ones to walk on this planet. So many have wanted to come, but places are limited. I have been a beacon of Light to many of you. I ask you to listen to me now. Do not doubt that it is me giving this message.

I, Jesus, have been blessed with your love and honoured by your prayers. It is now time for you to take your role in the world and lead by example. Would you want to be looked down upon by others around you? Then do not look down on those around you! For you are no better than others if you let your Ego assume superiority.

My love for you is as endless as the Universe. I wash my love over you and the planet, like soft raindrops across the world. My love cleanses. It heals. It breathes newness and creativity into the world like an unfurling petal on a spring morning.

I give this to you freely, but please ask for it. Ask for my help to make your hearts pure.

I am saddened by what is happening in the world. I gave up much to help the planet and its people. I suffered willingly for what I knew was my duty to God and my destiny, and I am saddened that it has come to this.

Do not shut this Manual and believe it to be the work of a person of simple mind, or of Ego, or pretence. Read this Manual and complete it with a passion – the passion you have for me, the passion I showed the world. For if you don't, you will have a strained and painful decade, with much suffering and loss. At worst, the world will cease to exist.

This is the message my father the Lord has given to you. Heed it, for we cannot be clearer than we are being now. I am going to give you a specific visualisation to do, one that will open your heart chakra and lift your vibrations. Perform this visualisation every day for one week. You will immediately see the difference.

I ask you to think of what you would be if you were the highest possible Self within yourself. If you were the Soul who looked upon me as an Equal, eye to eye, head high. Who would that person be? *Think on it now.* How would you need to change your life to become that person, that higher Soul? Write down what changes would be made. Now ask for my help to make those changes.

Laugh with joy at what you have. Laugh with joy that we in the celestial realms, what you call *Heaven*, are with you every step of the way. We love you; we are here to protect, guide and nurture you.

What we ask is that you nurture the planet and each other, the animals and plants and forests, the oceans; eat less meat, eat more vegetables; give blessings to whatever you eat, for you are truly blessed.

There is plenty in the world for all to eat, plenty for no person ever to go hungry. How can that be possible? Not by limiting yourself and being fearful, but by realising the love that goes into sharing, the honour that goes into releasing greed.

Enjoy fine things, but do not enjoy to excess, for where is the honour in that? I ask you to heed what your inner guidance tells you. Each of you has a Guardian Angel who works with your conscience. Listen, learn and act. Act NOW. Act for me, for our Lord, for the good of the planet and your future. Otherwise, there will not be a future to worry about.

It is I, Jesus, and I love you. Go with peace and prosperity, the prosperity of my love.

Message from Mother Mary

Dear beloved children, you are a great and vibrant people in a beautiful, beautiful world. I ask you to know and remember your connection to God. Know that I am with you every step you make. Call on me. Ask me to stand within you and my love and my strength will be within you, for I love humanity.

It is the heart that must open, for when the heart is open, love flows – love, understanding and compassion. With these qualities, no harm will come to the world, for people will care for and be tender with each other.

This is what I ask of you – of all of you. No matter how dark someone's nature may be, I ask you to see the light that burns within them. That is the light of our Lord and it is a light we all have within us, though sometimes it is very lost.

So delve deep within yourselves. I will help you find this light, for I love you. If you ask, I will be with you at all times, by your side, leading you where you should be going: back to the Lord. And this is not the Lord of a single religion, of Christianity or Catholicism over everything else. It is a Lord who shines down, loving all equally because He has created everyone on the planet.

There is no one right path and until you know this, you will not be enlightened and you will not find your way back to the Lord. My message is of love and understanding.

And for the women out there, know you are equal to men in every way. Your powers and qualities may not be similar, but as people, as humans, you stand equal.

Know your power, know your strength. Use it for the good of humanity and the planet, for if you do not speak out, things will not change.

You must speak out for what is good, what is right. You must protect the weak, you must protect your children, and you must protect the planet.

But protection does not mean living in fear. Protection means knowing that with love, with my love and the Lord's love, you will be protected from everything. And you always have our love. This is the greatest protection; it is peace itself.

Remember this, live this, and know that we will always look after you. Know you are Divinely loved. Know you are One with the Divine. That is my message to you, beloved children.

Message from Prophet Mohammed

I, the Prophet Mohammed, am tired of seeing people fight over religion and what I am supposed to have said or not said. I served the planet in love, unconditional love for all humans, irrespective of race, of gender, of seniority, of societal stature, and of creed.

It pains me to see people fight in my name. It is time for love. It is time for light to illuminate this beautiful planet, for sisters and brothers across races, cultures and creeds to take each other's hands and walk forward together in peace, harmony and cooperation.

For there is a bounty that the Divine kingdoms are willing to bestow upon the peoples of this world, if only they open their hearts to what is around them. For in fighting, in dogmatism, in thinking one religion is better than another, you do me an injustice. And you cut yourself off from Allah.

Allah is the pure flow of love that flows through every single one of us – and every single one of **you** on the planet. This love also flows through every part of the animal and plant kingdoms, the seas, oceans and forests.

Allah is pure love. And if you do not open yourself to this pure love, you cut yourself off from Allah, and you cut yourself off from me. That is my message.

Message from the Buddha

It is I, the Buddha. This is my message for the Manual. When I walked on the planet, few people could have imagined what the human race would become. There were people who behaved well and others not well. I gave them a direction, the direction of the higher, the better, the good.

It was a path of discipline, but also one of joy and laughter. That is why one of my forms is the Laughing Buddha. For life is about laughter, not malicious or with negative intent, but harmless, simple excitement about the mysteries of the world, the beauty of the world, the magnificence of the animal and plant kingdoms.

I am the last to give you a message for the Manual. And you will see a thread repeating itself throughout the messages: love the planet. For this is where it all begins and ends: loving the planet and its creatures.

If we had wanted you to stand alone, we could have put each of you on a separate planet in the Universe. Your challenge would have been to feed and shelter yourselves. But we didn't. We put you on this planet with millions of otherwise like-minded, lost Souls. Why? To learn how to live together, to learn how to help one another, to enjoy the company of each other, and to find forgiveness within yourselves and courage to stand up for what you know to be right.

This is where one of the flaws in humans has crept in, because too often you let the Ego decide what is right, rather than allowing the Inner Higher Self to speak out strongly about what is right. In a few Souls, the Ego is so powerful and the Higher Self so clouded by the Ego that they have no inner sense of conscience. But in most of you, the inner voice of reason, of love, of integrity is there.

If you are a person who takes what is not rightly yours from others, or from a company or the State, you know it is not right. The Ego will trick you into believing it is your inherent right to take such things. But your inner higher voice will tell you clearly it is wrong.

If you bully or brag, or are complicit in deeds of misconduct, the small voice in your head will tell you it is wrong. So I ask you no longer to subdue this voice; do not smother it with misplaced feelings of 'I deserve more…,' or, 'Others do this, so why can't I?' Allow your best and highest voice to speak out.

I will tell you a story about a small boy who always wanted what he didn't have. He had a very indulgent mother and whenever he asked for something, she gave it to him.

Eventually the mother became aware of the mounting pile of unused toys in his bedroom, and the string of clothes and bicycles that went untouched. She decided to stop giving him more and more. The little boy didn't accept that he had enough. He now started taking things from other children in the village. When they didn't give them to him, he used bullying tactics and took them forcefully.

As the boy grew up he became widely disliked, and upon adulthood he became an aggressive mob ruler. He thought nothing of taking life, if anyone stood in his way.

One day, his mother stood up and tried to stop him from taking the life of a woman who hadn't indulged his physical interest in her. The man killed his mother. Then he wept. He wept for all the things he had, which had brought him...what? Complete loneliness, widespread dislike and an unstoppable need for more.

At that point, the man decided to give everything away. He stood upon the ground where he had killed his beloved mother and kissed it. Then, adorning himself with plain clothes, he began wandering the planet, seeking an answer to his life, and how he could find inner peace and happiness. He knew it was not in belongings.

One day, he came upon a flowing river. Large rocks enabled travellers to cross it with ease. He sat upon a rock and felt the sun relax his face and body. A voice, gentle but persistent, which he had been ignoring for many years, now took the opportunity of his quiet mind and spoke clearly.

I am You. I am your best and highest Self and I love you. I love you dearly.

The man began to cry. How could such a beautiful voice say to him, an ogre who had killed his own mother, that he was lovable?

The voice replied, *Everyone is lovable, and you are as lovable as any. For you may have started out on a deviant path, but you have shown that you are able to feel, and love, and regret. Now you must show that you can forgive.*

As his tears rolled down his face into the stream, the man felt cleansed and loved. He knew what he had to do. He retraced his footsteps over the years, back to his village that he had left several years before and to the place where his mother had been killed by his own hand.

When he returned there, she was standing with love in her eyes and her hands outstretched. I have found you, he said. You have been found, she replied. You have found me by looking within yourself and finding You, your best and highest Self; your truth, your beauty, your connection to all that is good.

With that, the mother took her son's hand and lifted him to Heaven. In their place was a beautiful nectarine tree, full of bursting sweet fruit. It was the sweetness of joy, of love, of forgiveness. And it was said in many years to come that if one took a bite of the fruit of that tree, a person would find their best and highest Self. Then they would be incapable of malice, for the tree was pure goodness, the goodness we all have inside.

And that is my message to you beautiful humans: find your Soul, it is within you, and with your Soul, you will Ascend and join us in the celestial realms.

There are many paths to your Soul; be patient, be disciplined, but also find the joy. Transcend all fears and disbeliefs, transcend and become your Soul. I will greet you with open arms and a smiling face when you eventually Ascend. It is I, Buddha, and I thank you.

Message from Nelson Mandela, 'Madiba'

I have now passed over. It has been a miraculous journey, one I didn't realise could be made. Perhaps it is the biggest and greatest journey I have ever made. I now have a deeper understanding of my purpose in the life I have just completed.

At the time, something deep within me urged me on. I knew I had to be strong and courageous for my fellow countrymen and women. I knew I had to sever rage, anger and resentment for a higher goal that required achieving for the prosperity of all. Witnessing the decline of many countries in Africa, due to greed and power-hungry leaders, helped me unequivocally forgive, though not forget.

As I stand with you now, I reach out and brush you with the love I am now connected to. It is a beautiful place on this side of the veil. I am privileged to have contributed what I could to the Ascension of the planet whilst on Earth. Now I remain dedicated to the Earth's Ascension on this side of the veil. Whilst I miss my dear family and friends, I am with you. I watch and will you health and joy, just as I am constantly with all in South Africa, Africa and the world.

Work with me on the Ascension of Africa, in particular, to make Africa the shining light in the world that it needs to be. For Africa hosts the Earth's energetic spine. I know that now. Work with me, with hope in your heart, and I will work with you to bring health, wealth and enrichment to all, equally.

I am learning and in training myself, having just made the crossing, but I am ready for the challenge. With my love and gratitude to Source and the angelic kingdom, I thank you for reading these humble words and encourage you to complete and introduce the Manual into your daily lives.

Do not think I was pure or perfect. I wasn't. But I did my best and that is all we ask of you. Every day, do your best, and forgive yourself if you falter – keep trying, loving, forgiving.

❁ Visualisation from Jesus ❁

It is I, Jesus Christ. This is the visualisation I wish to give to you, my beloved creatures, for the benefit of your highest path and that of the planet. Use it frequently.

The more frequently you use it, the greater the impact it will have on your life and the more rapidly you will become a lightworker for the world – the greater will be your contribution to the planet, to my will and God's ultimate plan. We *want* you to work with us, but to do so, you must consciously decide to improve.

Feel your feet on the floor, close your eyes, and become aware of your breathing. Breathe deeply and evenly.

Become aware of a beautiful river flowing in front of you. This is the river of love. It is pure love and you feel the positive energy rippling off the skin of the water. You feel as though you are basking in sunlight, but really you are basking in the warmth of pure love.

The river is gentle. It meanders along and is just deep enough to allow you to submerge yourself fully.

Ask for me to appear by your side. With your Guardian Angel on the other side, we lead you into the water. You feel completely protected and safe. And as the water laps your ankles, you feel a wonderful exuberance roll up your legs and into your body, along your spine and into your head.

This is the exuberance of pure love. You gladly wade in more and more deeply, with your Guardian Angel and me by your side. The water has a tinge of gold and pink to it. These are the energies pure love releases in the seventh dimension, where I reside with the angels.

We keep walking more deeply into the water. Now it has reached your waist. You begin to remember good deeds you have done, the time you spent with someone in need, or someone who was lonely and wanted some company. These deeds that you carried out selflessly made you feel good about yourself, and you remember this feeling now.

We continue to walk into the river. Now it reaches your neck. You remember the deeds you did that were driven not by pure love, but by Ego, when you needed emotions from people around you to make you feel worthy. These memories bubble up in your mind, and you gladly release them, to be replaced with the pure love flowing around you.

It is now time to submerge yourself completely in the river of pure love. With your Guardian Angel holding your hand on one side and me on the other, we walk to the deepest part of the river of pure love.

We are completely submerged in water. But instead of holding our breath, we allow ourselves to inhale; and instead of water in our mouths, we inhale the most amazing energy.

It flows into our lungs, energising and healing them. It flows into our hearts and becomes a fountain of pink-gold energy.

As we continue to breathe in and out, the energy of pure love fills our bodies until our very blood and bones become pure love. We are pure love itself.

Whilst we are under the water, I turn to you and place my hand over your heart chakra, in the middle of your chest. I hold my hand there and you can feel the ultimate flow of love from me. For I am pure love and this is why my Father, God, Allah, Source, who is both male and female energies, gifted me to the Earth: so I could bring pure love to the planet.

It is my gift to you – God's gift – and in giving you the Christ Consciousness Energy, the energy of pure love, my energy, we gift through you pure love to the planet.

Carry it with humble pride. Wherever you walk for the next 24 hours, allow pure love to flow from you to all those around you.

It does not mean you need to be weak. Carry the Christ Consciousness Energy with your full strength and power dedicated to the joy and health of the world.

We now turn toward the bank of the river and walk easily and swiftly from the river of pure love, but you still feel the joy and exuberance of the Christ Consciousness Energy within you.

We greet you and will always be with you.

When you are ready, open your eyes and return to the room.

Example Timetable for Weeks 7 and 8

Activity	Week 7 by Day							Week 8 by Day						
	1	2	3	4	5	6	7	1	2	3	4	5	6	7
By this time, grounding and protection, invoking your Guardian Angel, and using the Golden Silver Violet flame and Mahatma Energy should be routine.														
You should have introduced the major changes to your diet and lifestyle, to live more harmoniously with nature.														
Continue to keep your journal as frequently as you can.														
Undertake the visualisation to connect with your Over-Lighting Master.														
Ask to be taken to the etheric retreat of an Ascended Master you feel close to.														
Choose a quality you want to enhance, e.g. courage, unconditional love, integrity or wisdom, and repeat the Alleluia Mantra.														
Undertake the Jesus visualisation every day for one week.														

Chapter 5

ANGEL ORBS

O rbs are My, Source's, gifts to you, beautiful children of My creation. I wanted you to have something tangible that you could see, as I'm aware of how difficult the Veil of Amnesia makes it for you to believe in the celestial kingdom.

These orbs are the energetic forms of My angels and other celestial beings in the seventh dimension and above – I say seventh and *above* because there are no limits in the celestial kingdom. Sometimes you will see an orb carrying a smaller orb, or even a face within the orb. This is because the angels routinely bring the Souls of deceased loved ones to you, to spend time with you, especially at important events like weddings, birthdays and graduations, parties and concerts.

At major concerts I send hosts of angels to raise the vibrations, for concerts can be major times of healing, as can events such as the Olympics and the World Cup. At these moments, the whole of the world is united in love and compassion for humankind. But we also send angels at these times to protect people from noise, and from negativity that may come from nationalistic pride.

Orbs will be wherever a celestial being is and as you become more closely linked to them, you will begin to recognise the blue-ringed orb of Archangel Michael, the orange orb of Prophet

Mohammed, and the rainbow and white orb of Archangel Butalyl. Each Archangel will resonate with a particular coloured orb.

Orbs may be different shapes at different times, even if sent by the same celestial being. This depends on the point of time the orb is captured, the energy levels of the person taking the photograph and the particular effect the celestial being wishes to have.

When they are captured on digital camera, they can be used thereafter to raise the vibrations of the person looking at the photograph. Certain orbs can aid Ascension, and we have captured some below to enable you to realise you are abundantly protected at all times. You just need to ask for protection from us.

Lastly, we have mentioned other celestial beings and spirit forms. Nature spirits and unicorns both have distinct orbs. The unicorn orbs are incredibly bright small orbs; nature spirit orbs are brilliant pinpricks. Enjoy them all.

Use the orbs for your enlightenment. Look at photographs of these orbs whilst in a state of unconditional love. The heart chakra and star chakra must be open for you to capture orbs on photo; the person taking the photo must be in a fifth dimensional state.

Each orb tells a story and will help in a different way toward enlightenment. Orbs can be meditated on or just looked at, but they hum with an energy that lifts off the page.

Trust that the orbs that come into your photos are the right ones for you. Ask for the best and highest orb to work with you and be open to what comes. Ask for a specific orb, maybe your Guardian Angel, or one of the Archangels – perhaps Michael or Gabriel – and see who comes.

The orbs of Archangels Michael, Butalyl and Chamuel were captured at the Luxor Temple in Egypt on the eleventh day of the eleventh month, 2011. Meditating on it will help with your Ascension (photo 1).

Photo 1: Archangel Michael, Butalyl and
Chamuel's orbs at Luxor Temple 11/11/2011

The Orb of Jesus

Photo 2: Wendy with the orb of Jesus (top right)

Photo 2 illustrates the power of ascended master orbs. The photo captures Wendy, an advanced psychic, and the orb of her Over-Lighting Master, Jesus (top right of centre, expanded in photo 3). Jesus's orb looks like a large moon and carries a smaller orb, which is the spirit of a deceased loved one. To the right-hand side of the photograph is the orb of Wendy's Guardian Angel.

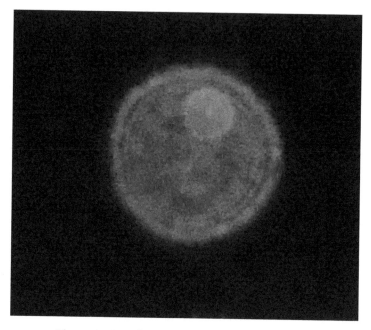

Photo 3: Angel orb of Jesus carrying spirit of
deceased loved one in a smaller orb within

Meditation on Jesus's Orb

Meditate on this orb of Jesus to connect more closely with the
Christ Consciouness Energy of unconditional pure love that Jesus
brought to Earth and still works with. It is essential to master
unconditonal love – respecting all humans without judgment –
and to Ascend to the sixth dimension. It is also essential to master
self-love.

Meditate on this orb photo and imagine a pink-gold flame of
love energy in your heart chakra. Imagine it growing and spread-
ing. It fills your body and your aura and continues to radiate to
all those you touch and come across. In this way, you will rapidly
progress to the sixth dimension.

Unicorn Orbs

Unicorns are seventh dimenional creatures that vibrate on the same frequency as angels. They are highly evolved horses. They do not exist on the physical plane currently, but as horses progress along their own spiritual path, they will eventually become unicorns in the celestial kingdom. They are fun-loving and drawn to the innocence and playfulness of children.

They are queuing up to work with you on your own spiritual journey and that of the world. Each of you has your own unicorn that I have gifted to you. Call on your unicorn to work with you along your spiritual journey. And if you have dedicated your life in some way to healing, improving or loving the world, multiple unicorns will be willing to work with you.

Meditate on the unicorn orbs captured in these photographs (photos 4 and 5) to Ascend more quickly, to have a closer psychic link to the animal kingdom, and to bring forth legions of these wise animals to work with you if you are dedicated to the best and highest path of the world.

Photo 1: Unicorn orbs and tiny nature spirit orbs in the snow

Photo 4: Enlargement of the Unicorn Orb in
the photo above (right-hand side by gate)

☼ Exercise ☼
Capture Angel Orbs

Try capturing your own angel orbs. It may help to perform a visualisation beforehand. Try taking the photo against a dark back-
ground, perhaps the garden at night, or at parties or weddings,
special occasions. It's often easier to capture orbs when you are
taking photos of your children and you are naturally in a loving
state of mind with them. Try calling in specific angels or Masters.

◉ Visualisation◉
To Help Capture Angel Orbs

Imagine you are standing on a quiet beach. The sand is firm
beneath your feet. The sea is calm before you. In the sea, not too
far from you, a boat floats. It comes toward you and you walk into
the ankle-high water and get into your boat.

Beside you, your Guardian Angel appears to keep you safe and protected on this journey. When you are comfortable inside the boat and sitting down, the boat moves of its own accord. It moves swiftly and smoothly across the calm blue sea.

You see land ahead. It is emerald green and gleaming, as though made of gemstones. As you approach, you realise the land is your home. This is where you were born and you feel an instant attachment.

You climb out of the boat and onto the shore. The sand has a beautiful golden radiance that makes you feel humbled.

The grass is thick, soft and firm beneath your feet as you leave the beach and walk on the land. Your Guardian Angel walks with you. If you are nervous, your Guardian Angel envelops you in his or her wings. You feel completely safe and loved.

In the centre of the land is a tree; beneath this tree is a bench. Sit on this bench. Your Guardian Angel sits with you. As you sit there, you feel the branches of the tree extend in all directions and reach outward and upward, toward the sky.

Beneath your feet, you feel the roots of the tree burrow deeply into the Earth. You feel yourself grow into the trunk of the tree. It feels good. You are taking on the power of this immense, wise tree. You become one with the roots of the tree, bonding you to the Earth and allowing you to feel deeply connected with it.

Your arms stretch outward and upward with the branches of the tree. You feel your star and crown chakras open to the wisdom of the heavens your branches are stretching to.

Above you, a beautiful white light shines from the blue sky. It gets brighter and brighter. You realise this light is the wisdom and love of the celestial kingdom: the Heaven you imagine to be the most beautiful place in existence.

You are now ready to accept Heaven on Earth. The light descends into your top chakras, through the crown, third eye, throat, heart, solar plexus, sacral, root and into your Earth star chakra, about 30cm beneath your feet.

Your whole body lights up with a warm vibrant glow: the glow of the celestial world. You feel blessed, nurtured, loved, powerful and beneficent. The glow lasts several minutes.

When you are ready, you step easily away from the tree but retain its power and wisdom. Your Guardian Angel takes you by the hand and leads you back to the boat, across the water and to the beach, where you first started.

You now know your true connection to the Divine and to the Earth. When you are ready, become aware of your breathing, feel your feet on the ground and open your eyes.

Example Timetable for Weeks 9 and 10

Activity	Week 9							Week 10						
	1	2	3	4	5	6	7	1	2	3	4	5	6	7
By this time, grounding and protection, invoking your Guardian Angel, and using the Golden Silver Violet flame and Mahatma Energy should be routine.														
You should have introduced the major changes to your diet and lifestyle to live more harmoniously with nature. Praise yourself for your newly achieved lifestyle.														
Meditate on the Luxor Temple orbs and ask to be taken to the retreat of Serapis Bey, the Ascended Master whose etheric retreat is above the temple.														
Undertake the visualisation to help capture orbs.														
Experiment with photographing angel orbs around people and calling in different celestial beings or loved ones.														

Chapter 6

CUTTING NEGATIVE TIES

In the beginning, I decided to recreate Myself in thought forms that I sent out to experience existence in new ways. The part of Me that I sent out became Soul Groups consisting of individual parts, human beings amongst other life forms. Soul Groups can consist of beings from different planets, not just Earth.

I keep one part of the Soul Group with Me at all times, while the other eleven parts are sent forth to experience life in different realms and planets. This is somewhat simplified, but generally each Soul Group includes twelve Souls, each in turn comprised of twelve parts.

One part of the Soul always remains with the Soul Group. The other eleven parts go forth and experience.

I connect to you all through your Soul Groups (otherwise known as the Monad); and through the Soul Group, to your Soul.

Each of you is one Aspect of a Soul. There are 144 Soul Aspects in each Soul Group (Monad).

Before their first incarnation on Earth, a Soul will sit with their Guardian Angel and the Archangel Gabriel and discuss the lessons that need to be learnt on this planet.

Each Soul will have full awareness of their best and highest path, or 'blueprint' for existence. This is the essence of all that is good in the person and the highest potential they can attain throughout all incarnations.

Following each incarnation, there will be a reassessment of the most essential lessons that need learning, and Soul contracts will be signed between Souls based around the lessons to be learned in the forthcoming incarnation.

The most significant Soul contracts are those with parents and close family members, including children.

A Soul may agree to sign a Soul contract for two reasons: first, because they have karma to repay, and second, because they have lessons they must learn and / or there is a reciprocal 'helping out', e.g. 'I'll help you learn your lessons if you help me learn mine.'

Often Souls will sign Soul contracts with the same Souls over many incarnations. This is a form of 'Soul family', but recognise it is not the same as the parts of your 'Soul' or the Monad. Souls from the same Monad, or various parts of the same Soul, infrequently sign a Soul contract together.

Because of the Veil of Amnesia, humans have no recollection of these Soul contracts once they have incarnated.

As you can imagine, if the Veil of Amnesia didn't exist and there were full memory, it would be very easy to forgive, love unconditionally and honour the people with whom you have Soul contracts. Very little learning would take place.

As it is, the Veil of Amnesia ensures that the Soul Contracts do just what they are supposed to do: tax people to the fullest, and create situations so challenging that either the Souls do not overcome the lesson for many lifetimes, or they do manage to overcome the challenge and a vast leap in spiritual growth is achieved.

Have you been in a marriage where your partner constantly presses your buttons? Makes you irate when with other people you are calm and collected? Or are you in a relationship where you feel unloved and disregarded?

Your partner and those closest to you are your best teachers. Therefore, stop being angry with the people you may initially see as inflicting hurt or dishonour upon you and recognise them for what they are: your best teachers.

Being aware that someone challenging is helping you learn your life lessons does not mean that you should accept their treatment without asserting yourself. It does not mean you should stay in a relationship that is abusive or harmful. However, it does allow you to understand the deeper Soul level dimensions of your key relationships, and hopefully it gives you increased ability to forgive them even if it is necessary to move on.

Look more deeply into the situation. The experience on the outside most likely mirrors a lesson you have to learn on the inside. If your child has withdrawn from you, causing you to feel unloved and rejected, recognise the part of you that feels unworthy of love.

Recognise the part of you that is hard on yourself, self-critical and judgmental of your own actions. Now, having recognised this part of yourself that is creating a toxic environment within your body, counteract it.

How do you do this? By giving yourself love energy, honour and respect, praising yourself for your achievements. Accept and deeply feel that you are at exactly the right stage in your life, for the afterlife does not reward a person for being the best or the highest-paid, or top in an organisation. It rewards you for your spiritual growth and the lessons you have learnt.

What lessons do you still need to learn? Do you honour, love, nurture and cherish yourself and those around you?

Do you regard all people in the world as equals, whether they be a murderer, a robber or stingy with their money?

Do you look down on people who do not dress as well or have less money or status than you? Does a part of you feel (or want to feel) superior?

Become aware, and in this awareness, you take back the power from the Ego. You take a leap along your own path of self-awareness and spiritual growth.

By recognising this is just a part of you, floating at the surface, you take the step in the fifth dimension and are well on your way to Ascension.

We will now undertake a powerful visualisation to release negative attachments to people, places or things that are holding you back.

People are often aware they have negative associations with other people. However, you may also have negative associations with a particular place or object. For instance, a person who has been in a traumatic car accident may have a negative association with driving.

This visualisation can help sever those ties and assist with the healing process.

When you recognise you are energetic as well as physical bodies, it becomes apparent that you can remain energetically connected to a person or place, even if you do not physically see them.

For instance, energetic cords may remain between lovers, partners or others with whom you have been in intense relationships, whether these relationships were based on sex, work, family or friendship.

Depending on the type of negative attachment that exists, the cord may originate from a particular chakra. It is also worth being aware that cords can remain attached to spirits of people who have passed away or entities that may have become lodged in your aura.

Therefore, when performing the visualisation, do not have a predetermined idea of who or what should appear for the ties to be cut. Trust that whatever comes is what needs to be cut.

Entities usually mean no harm; they are simply energy forms that do not exist on the Earthly plane. However, they may inadvertently draw your energy. This is why it is important to give them love energy, as love is the greatest healer. It is also why working with the angels is so powerful in cutting your energetic cords.

Be aware of where the cord exits your body. If it leaves from your solar plexus, the lesson to be learned may relate to power and status in the world or within a relationship. If a cord leaves from the heart chakra, it is related to the lack of unconditional love you give to yourself, as well as the unconditional love you must allow to flow for the person or within the world.

◈ Visualisation◈
To Cut Negative Attachments

Relax. Close your eyes and become aware of your breathing. Feel your feet on the floor and tiny roots growing into the Earth, grounding you. Feel Archangel Michael place you in a ball of his blue protective energy, protecting you 100%.

You are now in a beautiful, sacred place. Breathe in the fresh air and feel it on your skin. You feel comfortable and safe.

Beside you, on your left, appears the Archangel Michael. On your right appears your Guardian Angel. They will be with you as you cut the cords of attachment to people, places or things that are holding you back.

Become aware of a brown cord of energy emanating from your body. Take time to become aware of what the cord is attached to. Be aware of any emotions you associate with this attachment.

Give the person, place or thing love. Feel unconditional love for it radiating out from your heart chakra. Continue to give it unconditional love until it is surrounded by a pink ball of light.

Listen to any messages that come to you about this attachment.

Give thanks for the lesson you have had to learn.

Now Archangel Michael takes his sword of light and raises it above the cord connecting you to the person, place or thing. His sword of light cuts through the cord like butter.

If there is more than one cord, his sword slices through all of them easily.

Now Archangel Michael and your Guardian Angel place their hands over the areas of your body where the cords emerged. They send healing energy into these places, completely sealing and healing the emotions that existed.

They do the same for the person, place or thing and, as they do so, the person, place or thing disappears.

Give thanks to the Archangel Michael and your Guardian Angel. When you are ready, feel your feet on the floor, become aware of your breathing and return to the room.

The following visualisation to understand the Soul contracts you have with your parents is a very powerful one. It can be repeated with a biological father or mother, a step-parent or parent through adoption. You can repeat this visualisation replacing a parent with another significant person in your life.

◎ Visualisation◎
To Understand the Soul Contracts with Your Parents

Feel your feet firmly on the floor. Feel tiny golden roots leave the soles of your feet and burrow into the soil, grounding you to Mother Earth.

Ask Archangel Michael to protect you in a ball of his blue energy of protection.

Ask your Guardian Angel to wrap their wings around you, protecting you 100%.

You find yourself in a grassy meadow. The sun is warm but gentle, and butterflies flit across the colourful flowers around you.

To your left is a meandering river. As you watch, a golden barge threads its way along the river and stops beside you. Upon it is a shining figure.

The figure steps off the barge and you recognise it as your father's highest Self, all that is good and wonderful within your father.

You greet your father and he comes to meet you. Ask your father what life lessons he is helping you learn, as agreed in your Soul contract with him.

Listen to what he has to say and ask any additional questions you may have. When you have finished, thank him and send him unconditional love. Also receive the unconditional love he sends you.

He now steps onto the golden barge and it sails away.

Around the bend in the river, another barge appears. It is made of rubies and rich gemstones. There is a beautiful shining figure upon this barge. As it gets closer, you see this figure is the best and highest Self of your mother.

The barge stops beside you and your mother descends. You greet your mother's highest Self and ask her what lessons she agreed to help you learn in your Soul contract.

Listen to what she says and ask any additional questions you may have. When you have finished, send her unconditional love energy and receive it from her.

Thank her. Bid her farewell, and watch as she steps back onto the barge and sails away.

When you are ready, become aware of your breathing. Rub your fingers with your thumbs and open your eyes.

◈ Visualisation ◈
To Release All Negativity

Imagine you are in a cool forest. The trees above your head create a green and golden pattern with the sunlight. It is now time for you to take off the robe of neediness.

You will have been carrying this robe on your back for many years. It is the accumulation of all the times you have felt alone, abandoned, and only happy when surrounded by others.

This is not the good part of having friends and loved ones. This is the needy part that stops you standing in your full power as an Ascended Master, full of love and light.

You become aware of a weight across your shoulders. It is not a pleasant weight. You realise you have been carrying this weight around for many years.

You have experienced many unhealthy emotions at work and home, when you wanted people to respond to you in particular ways and, when they didn't, you felt angry, unloved, vulnerable, rejected, abandoned.

This cloak is a dirty green colour and it has splotches where particularly bad emotions have dragged you down.

It is now time to discard this cloak. Ask for the assistance of your Guardian Angel. Feel the presence of this beautiful angel beside you.

Now unclasp the clip holding the cloak around your neck. With the help of your Guardian Angel, let the cloak fall to the floor and step away from it.

Feel the new sense of weightlessness. Become aware of the light and joy in your body and the pure love in your heart.

Turn around and look down at the cloak as it lies on the ground.

Ask Archangel Zadkiel to place it in the Golden Silver Violet flame. Watch as it turns to a golden rainbow and disappears.

Now know your full power to stand on your own, with the knowledge that you are never alone, because I am always within you.

Example Timetable for Weeks 17 and 18

Activity	Week 17							Week 18						
	1	2	3	4	5	6	7	1	2	3	4	5	6	7
Ground and protect yourself every day. Use the Golden Silver Violet flame and the Source or Mahatma Energy every day.	░	░	░	░	░	░	░	░	░	░	░	░	░	░
Visualisation to cut negative attachments.	░													
Visualisation to understand Soul contracts.				░										
Visualisation to release all negativity.									░					

Note: These visualisations can be repeated as necessary.

Chapter 7

THE SOURCE ENERGY

There are many energies from the Divine kingdom available for human use at this time. You have been introduced to the Mahatma Energy and the Golden Silver Violet flame. You are also aware that you can use Archangel Gabriel's white light of purification to cleanse and Archangel Raphael's light to heal you. Archangel Michael is there for your protection and that of your loved ones.

You can draw Archangel Chamuel's energy through you to heal your heart chakra and attain pure love.

Many of the Ascended Masters also work with a particular energy, such as the Christ Consciousness (Mary Magdalene and Jesus) and St Germain (the Golden Silver Violet flame). Ray o' Light works with the light of fearlessness; call on his light if you want courage and strength.

You can access the energy of any of the celestial beings in the Divine Kingdom. You can also access the energy of wise trees and plants on your planet, of wise animal spirits and high-vibration creatures you are not familiar with on Earth but who are willing to work with you to raise your vibrations.

So much I as Source have gifted you, for your personal development and so you can save the beloved Earth upon which you live. But there is only one energy that is My personal energy. Every energy on this planet flows from the connection with Me. But My pure energy is the Source Energy, and I gift this to you now.

The Source Energy is even more powerful than the Mahatma Energy and, in itself, will enable everyone to Ascend, even those stuck in the third dimension.

It will reverse climate change; it will heal all toxins in the sea. It is mightily powerful. It is guarded by **Me**. It is My own energy and I give it to you.

I shall now take you through a visualisation to bring through the Source Energy. To use this energy, a person must already have committed to helping the Earth in some way. If they have not, they should not use this energy.

For most people, I cannot allow the full power of the energy to flow through them immediately; but with repeated access to the Source Energy, and as their vibrations raise, they will be able to hold the full power of the energy.

This energy will give people advanced psychic skills that they can awaken *when* and *only* when they are ready. We shall begin.

⚙ Visualisation⚙
To Bring Through the Source Energy

Ground and protect yourself.

Imagine your star chakra is filled with a multi-coloured light that pulses with the power of a thousand stars. Feel the beauty. Move the light clockwise.

Now pull the power down into your crown chakra. The multi-coloured light with the power of a thousand stars now fills your crown chakra and moves clockwise. It heals, it cleanses, it energises, it reconfigures all that has been before into all that is from now on.

Now pull the energy into your third eye. The multi-coloured light of a thousand stars spins clockwise. It is bright, it is beauitiful, it is the energy of Source and it is given with love.

The multi-coloured energy of a thousand stars moves into your throat and into your heart. You feel your heart chakra expand

and blossom like the petals of the most beautiful flower, and it spins clockwise.

My energy moves into your solar plexus, expanding that area, filling it with the multi-coloured light with the power of a thousand stars that spins clockwise.

Now pull the energy into your sacral. Feel the multi-coloured energy expand wtih the power of a thousand stars. Feel whole, feel loved. The energy spins clockwise.

Now pull this light into your root and feel your root expand with the power of a thousand stars. Spin it clockwise.

Draw it down into your Earth star chakra, 30cm below your feet. Feel it expand with the power of a thousand stars. Spin it clockwise.

Now pull the energy down into the Earth's core, so the core of Mother Earth throbs with the power of a thousand stars and the beautiful multi-coloured light spreads out through the Earth, through the atmosphere, through the Universe. The connection is complete.

I will pour the full force of the energy through you and into the Earth, healing it, loving it, creating it as an Ascended Earth – creating you as an Ascended Master, standing in your full power.

The Source Energy is the most powerful energy ever given to the planet, more powerful than any energy gifted during the time of Atlantis, and I have given it to you to bring to the Earth. It is the energy of creation, the energy of manifestation, the energy of pure love. It will be useless for those who wish to do harm or use it for their own Ego.

Example Timetable for Weeks 11 and 12

Activity	Week 11							Week 12						
	1	2	3	4	5	6	7	1	2	3	4	5	6	7
Ground and protect yourself every day.														
Use the Source Energy every day, morning and evening. The first time the Source Energy is accessed, follow the visualisation as described in this chapter. Thereafter, a shortened version can be used on a regular basis with wording as follows: 'I call on the Source Energy to flow through my body and my aura into the core of the Earth, connecting me to the Divine.'														
Write in your Angel journal any feelings or changes you experience.														

Chapter 8

RELEASING FULL KARMA

This is My message about karma. I keep a balance sheet for each one of you. The balance sheet is a record of all your good and bad deeds in every life you lead.

At the end of each life, your Soul leaves your physical body. For most of you, rather than this being a difficult challenge, it is freeing; you realise you are an energy being rather than a physical being, the body being like a container for the Soul in that particular lifetime.

The Soul is often confused at this stage unless close to or already Ascended, but the celestial kingdom sends many helpers to enable you to pass over smoothly.

Archangel Azrael, the angel of death, will be there to accompany you to the other side, and more often than not the Soul will be met by a plethora of Soul friends and family who await the new arrival at their Homecoming.

For that is what it is: a great celebration to welcome the Soul home. I do not visit personally unless you have Ascended, but there will be wise Souls and angelic helpers to meet and greet all of the newly passed-over Souls.

Very soon after passing over, the Soul will be brought to the Lords of Karma, who sit on the Karmic Board. This is where all the good and bad deeds over previous incarnations are assessed.

This is a wonderful, empowering ceremony, conducted in close discussion with the Soul and the Soul's Guardian Angel. The Soul feels the power of pure love and lack of judgment of the Board.

The Board itself is comprised of evolved, wise Masters and celestial beings appointed especially for their judgment, pure love and wisdom. Presently there are eight members of the Karmic Board. These are:

- the Great Divine Director, who holds the blueprint of each of your Souls within him;
- Lady Nada, the Great Keeper of the Soul Keys;
- Pallas Athena, the Goddess of Truth;
- Elohim Cyclopea, who focuses the action of the all-seeing eye of God;
- Lady Portia, Goddess of Justice;
- Kuan Yin, Goddess of Mercy;
- the Goddess of Liberty; and
- Lady Gaia, protector of the Earth's animal and plant kingdoms. She has been invited to join because of the importance of looking after the planet, in order for a Soul to Ascend. It reflects the difficult times the Earth is experiencing through the heavy hand and exploitation of many humans.

You will have to stand witness to all of these powerful Masters and celestial beings. I have given you important dispensations regarding your karma in recent years. Now you only need to balance 51% of your karmic debt in order to Ascend. A lifetime of good deeds in this life can therefore enable you to Ascend. I have also bestowed upon you the Golden Silver Violet flame, which can be used to transmute negative karma instantly, meaning you don't have to collect additional karma in this lifetime.

This is not to say you can go around committing bad deeds, thinking the Golden Silver Violet flame can be used to nullify the karma. The celestial kingdom keeps a careful eye on all indiscretions and will negate the Golden Silver Violet flame's power for those who misuse it.

Many light-workers will collect no more karma in this lifetime because they have mastery over their deeds and the small mistakes they make are nullified with the flame.

What of people who do not cancel out the karma? Either they return in another incarnation to experience the tests again, or if they have shown an insurmountable level of badness across many lifetimes, we will send them to be purged and cleansed. This is a blessing for them and for the Universe. If they do not show repentance, they will not rise again but will remain as ash. Know there is no evil; there is only the choice of a human.

What do I classify as a bad deed? I do not need to tell most of you what would fall into this category, but I will give some examples: indecencies with children, torture of humans or animals, war, and the killing of innocents who cannot protect themselves and who have done you no direct harm. These are the worst forms of sin.

All harmful thoughts should be harnessed and replaced with pure and loving thoughts. We understand moderate transgressions are part of the learning process, but we ask you to strive for unconditional pure love in your hearts.

And we tell you to judge no one; it is only for *Me* and the Karmic Board to judge. For you know not what is in another's Soul contract. Even Souls who have committed acts as heinous as those listed above may be carrying out the provisions of a Soul contract in order for others to learn their lessons. This may have been with our agreement.

It is the Souls who have conducted these misdeeds out of their own free will, irrespective of the Soul contract they have signed, who will find the Karmic Board loving but unable to overlook their actions.

Lastly, I would ask that if you have committed a wrongdoing, forgive yourself. If you fully repent, we will allow your karma to be transmuted in the Golden Silver Violet flame. But if you forgive yourself with the intent to wrong again, we shall know.

⚙ *Visualisation* ⚙
With the Great Divine Director

Close your eyes and feel your feet firmly on the ground. You are standing in front of a golden table. On the table is a map. It is the map of your life.

You approach the table to look at the map, and you are greeted by the Great Divine Director.

He picks up the map and hands it to you. But the page is fuzzy and you cannot see clearly what the mission of your life is. What is your highest potential?

The Great Divine Director hands you a pair of jewelled spectacles. They are very light and fine.

When you place them on the bridge of your nose, the map of your life suddenly becomes clear. You see the purpose of your life and your highest potential.

You realise the importance of where you are right now in your learning.

Thank the Great Divine Director and know that you are on your best and highest path from now on. When you are ready, return to the room and open your eyes.

⚙ *Visualisation* ⚙
Petition the Karmic Board to Release All Karma

Close your eyes. Feel your feet firmly on the ground. Now ask for protection from Archangel Michael. He wraps his cloak around you.

You find yourself in the glade of a forest. Around you, great trees rise up, tall and commanding. The glade is full of soft pink flowers. You smell the scent of the flowers: it is like honey and nectarines.

Breathe deeply and evenly.

In front of you stands your Guardian Angel. They wrap their wings around you and effortlessly lift you upward, over the trees, so you are flying high over the tops, completely safe and secure.

You see a magnificent white castle in the distance and, very quickly, you near the castle. Your Guardian Angel lowers you gently to the ground, where a unicorn waits to escort you inside the castle.

The castle is made from white marble and it gleams in the morning sunshine. As you follow the unicorn, you realise you are entering a grand central hallway.

In front of you is a long wide table. At the table sit the celestial beings who will review your karmic records. This is the Karmic Board.

It consists of both distinguished men and women: Ascended Masters who through their wisdom, pure love, judicial opinion and compassion have been selected for this most important event.

You ask the Head of the Board if they will consider your petition to release all karmic debt up to today and, from this day, the ability to release your karma instantly as you create it.

The Head of the Board asks if you can write down all the wrong deeds you have done in this lifetime.

He provides you with a pen and parchment and you sit on a comfortable chair to write.

Your Guardian Angel helps you write down misdeeds from previous lives that have accumulated karmic debt and need to be released. When you have finished, you hand over the parchment.

The Chair of the Board passes your petition along the line of distinguished Ascended Masters.

Listen for any advice or guidance they might give you. Respond if they ask you any questions.

If you do not have true love in your heart and the determination to become a better person, they will see this. If you do not seriously seek to become a better person, your karmic debt will not be completely cleared.

Your Guardian Angel now asks on your behalf for the Karmic Board's decision.

Listen to their response.

They now send Archangel Zadkiel to stand over you and surround you in the Golden Silver Violet flame. Now all karmic debt that is ready to be lifted from this life and all previous lives will be lifted.

Become aware of any sensations you may feel. Thank Archangel Zadkiel and the Karmic Board humbly.

Enjoy the sensation as your Guardian Angel leads you back through the castle, following the unicorn, and then wraps you in his wings and flies you over the trees, back to the glade in the forest. Thank your Guardian Angel.

When you are ready, return to the present. Shrug your shoulders. Feel the floor underneath your feet and open your eyes.

Example Timetable for Weeks 13 and 14

Activity	Week 11							Week 12						
	1	2	3	4	5	6	7	1	2	3	4	5	6	7
Ground and protect yourself every day. Use the Golden Silver Violet flame and the Source or Mahatma Energy every day.														
Undertake the visualisation with the Great Divine Director.														
Undertake the visualisation to petition the Karmic Board to release all karma.														

Chapter 9

HEALING YOUR BODIES OF DISEASE

Disease is the opposite of 'ease'. When you don't look after your bodies, you put them out of alignment and this causes *dis*ease. Even when you look after your bodies, sometimes it is simply part of your Soul contract, or your best and highest path, to experience the disease. However, many of you reading this Manual will not be taking enough care of your bodies and that is something completely within your control.

Do you smoke? Do you regularly drink large quantities of alcohol? Do you take drugs, prescription or non-prescription? Do you carry major stress on your shoulders without trusting that we will help you manage the stressful situations? Or are you struggling against challenges in your life rather than giving in to the natural flow of your life, focusing on positive affirmations and working with us to help carry you through? All these things will tire and debilitate your body, and they should be addressed.

I wish you to become far more communicative with your bodies. Most of you have forgotten that your bodies are wise and know most of the answers you seek. Your bodies can also tell you what is good or not good to ingest. Use your intuition, your innate wisdom, to listen to your bodies and understand how to keep them in peak health.

Also be aware that the angelic kingdom doesn't like smoke, and that smoking tobacco and drinking alcohol reduces your vibrations. Likewise, a poor diet with high-cooked fats and synthetic beverages reduces your vibrations. We are not saying these are morally wrong, just that they are not good for your bodies, especially in large quantities and high frequency. You should consider what this means for your Ascension.

You are energetic bodies, as well as physical bodies. Your auras extend far beyond the physical boundaries of your bodies and disease starts in the auric field before it actually manifests in your physical bodies. Some advanced energy healers can see the disease as fractures, blocks or weaknesses in the aura before any physical symptom is perceived. This is why energy healing can be a very powerful way to improve and prevent maladies and disease. Preventive action is the path to Ascension.

It is also important for you to embrace the reality that many diseases and maladies are there to teach you a lesson with an emotional or spiritual underpinning. We shall look at these in more detail within this chapter. But for those of you reading this who believe illness is there to be treated with conventional medicine from the chemist without looking more deeply into the underlying cause, I want you to pause and realise that prevention will require you to look deeply within your consciousness; access your subconscious, as this is where your highest path lies.

For those of you who have tried many healing approaches that have not worked, it may be that you have chosen your malady for the lesson it teaches you, or for the strength you can gain through the challenges you are faced with. Your strength can shine like a beacon of light to those around you and be the fuel for Ascension.

This is an exciting voyage: the voyage of the body, the voyage of the Self. I have created you all as amazing complex mechanisms that require oiling at every level – mind, body, spirit – to be whole, to be vital, to be Ascended Masters standing in your full power. For some of you, this chapter will be nothing new; for others, it will open up a realm that is truly fascinating. Have fun discovering yourselves.

Measuring Your Chakras

To understand why misalignment may occur at the energetic level, we return to the questions of life purpose and the lessons you have to learn. As I introduced in Chapter 1, chakras – meaning 'wheels' or 'disks' in Sanskrit – are energy centres within your bodies. They are the points of maximum energy intake. If your chakras are out of balance, your whole energy field is out of balance. Each chakra links to a particular layer of your aura, also known as your light-body. Chakras also link to specific body parts, emotions and issues.

To measure your chakras, you can take a pendulum and hold it above the point of the chakra and about 30cm away from the body. Allow the movement of the chakra to pull the pendulum in a particular direction or shape.

If there is no movement at all, this means the chakra is blocked or the energy stagnant. If the chakra spins clockwise, this suggests the chakra is open and healthy.

If it spins anticlockwise, there are likely to be negative associations with that chakra. These can be ascertained by understanding the 'issues' associated with that chakra.

For instance, a strongly anticlockwise spin in the sacral chakra could suggest issues relating to sexuality and / or lack of creativity. If this continues over a long period, it could lead to physical problems of the prostate / bladder, lower-back issues, or even frigidity and impotence.

By working on the aura, and cleansing and energising the chakras, physical ailments can often be avoided. If they do manifest, one possible reason is that issues relating to that chakra have not been adequately dealt with. Another possible reason is that it may be in your Soul contract to experience this particular challenge or ailment. In such cases, working on cleansing the chakra will still enable Ascension, even if the condition is not addressed.

☼ Exercise ☼

Measuring Your Chakras – 2 People or More

One person should lie down on a bed, massage table or the floor. A second person should hold a pendulum over each chakra in the person's body. Draw the shape the pendulum makes on a piece of paper. Be clear what direction the pendulum follows.

If the pendulum swings anticlockwise, the chakra is out of balance; if the chakra swings clockwise, the chakra is healthy. Be aware of how wide the chakra spins. A very small spin indicates a low flow of energy through the chakra. An erratic spin could indicate out of control energy in this area. Ideally, the pendulum will spin in a perfect clockwise circle.

To measure the crown and star chakras, ask the person to sit upright and hold the pendulum above the person's head, first 10cm and then 30cm above.

Archangels and Chakras

I have asked a number of My Archangels to work specifically on guarding and guiding the chakras within the body and within the planet Earth. These Archangels have been chosen for their abilities and their resonance with the chakra they work with.

Sandolphon

Sandolphon is a mighty Archangel who guards and guides the Earth star chakra. The Earth star chakra enables a human to reach their full potential, and to bring the Divine knowledge and light into the Earth to manifest in the physical.

Sandolphon has been chosen for his strength, groundedness, love of the plant and animal kingdoms, and for his ability to teach across the spectrum of species within the Universe. Sandolphon is like My anchor, the anchor of the Universe, and he roots you to the Earth through your Earth star chakra. Work with him and visit his etheric retreat in Jordan.

Gabriel

Gabriel is a beloved Archangel of mine and works closely by My side. Gabriel is the angel of creativity, affiliated with writers and journalists. She works with both the root / base and the sacral (and naval) chakras.

Gabriel is the angel of purification. Her angels clean up much of the mess in the world when asked to do so. Her white light of purification is incredibly powerful.

Work with Gabriel to feel grounded to the Earth, to know your ability to survive is at My command. Gabriel will help you create your own reality, master the Law of manifestation, and enjoy your sexuality and sensuality, as long as it doesn't contravene the bonds of marriage. Visit her etheric retreat between Sacramento and Mount Shasta, California, USA.

Uriel

Uriel is the angel of fearlessness and mercy. She is an angel of magnificent strengths and versatility. She works closely with the solar plexus chakra, where many humans store the weaknesses of their Ego. Uriel is on hand to give you the fearlessness and strength to overcome anxieties you may have in relationships, whether they be with partners, friends or in a work context. Her angels are always available to remind you that you are an amazing being. Visit Uriel in her etheric retreat in the Tatra Mountains, South of Cracow, Poland.

Chamuel

My Archangel of the heart chakra, Chamuel gives her pure love to you, for your salvation. If you embrace the love within you, and connect to My Divine love flowing through all living things on the planet, you will own happiness and Heaven on Earth will be yours. Go to Chamuel's etheric retreat in Mount Sinai.

Michael

Already beloved to many of you reading this, Michael is the warrior Archangel and he leads legions of angels of protection. Michael works closely with the throat chakra, for it is through the throat that humans express much of their turmoil, anxiety and Ego-related emotions and failings. But if you speak clearly with love and light, your throat chakra will be a channel for Divine knowledge, wisdom and transcendence. Visit Michael in his etheric retreat in Banff and Lake Louise, Canada.

Raphael

Raphael is the Archangel of healing. She is a beautiful and powerful angel who leads millions of angels who have devoted their spiritual path to healing. She works closely with those dedicated to healing others. If you wish to heal a malady in the body, turn to Raphael. Visit her etheric retreat in Mesopotamia, where she has moved to give love and healing.

Jophiel

Jophiel is a wise and astute Archangel who works particularly with the crown chakra. He spends much time transmuting My energy and bringing it to a level most humans can tolerate. The crown is the doorway to the body, and Jophiel works to keep the crown chakra open and cleansed, as well as the whole of the aura. Jophiel specialises in peace. Visit Jophiel's etheric retreat south of the Great Wall of China near Lanchow, North-Central China.

Metatron

Metatron is the greatest of the Archangels because of the experiences he has had, both human and angelic. He and his brother Sandolphon are the only two Archangels who have previously experienced a physical body, although I am now sending many angels into physical bodies to raise the vibrations of Earth more rapidly.

Metatron is the Archangel of Africa, for that continent needs additional help to raise its vibrations both because it has been mired in the negative use of energy by humans throughout the ages and because of its critical role in the Ascension of the planet. With Metatron's help, Africa will rise great and powerful, as is her due.

Metatron guards and guides the star chakra and connects directly with My energy, drawing My Divine energies through the star and passing it down to the other chakras, eventually connecting with the centre of the Earth. In this way, My Divine light is drawn to Earth. Work with Metatron and visit his etheric retreat in Giza, Egypt.

The Power to Heal Your Bodies

All of these Archangels and their angels can enable you to keep your chakras cleansed and powerful. And through keeping your chakras healthy, you will keep you body healthy and your Soul on its path to Ascension.

Guard your thoughts, for negative thoughts result in energetic forms that lead to malady and, if left unhealed, disease. You have the power to heal your body of any maladies or disease, unless it is in your Soul contract to experience as part of your own Ascension challenge or provide a lesson for others to learn by.

Even if in your Soul contract you have chosen a particular path that includes certain physical conditions, working on the chakras with My Archangels will enable you to Ascend and join Me directly. Be happy, try to be healthy, love your bodies and your minds, go easy on yourselves and find inner peace with the helpers I have sent you. See table 4 and figure 2 for the key information linked to the chakras.

Table 4 **The Human Energy Field and Chakras in the Fifth Dimension**

Chakra	Archangel	Energy Field of the Body	Parts of Physical Body Influenced	Chakra Out of Balance[1]	Chakra Balanced[2]	Related Crystals and Essential Oils
Star	Metatron	Divine	Psychological influence	Megalomania, bipolar, schizophrenia	Pure connection with Source	Selenite Oil of Violet
Crown	Jophiel	Ketheric	Right brain and pineal gland	Alzheimer's, confusion, paranoia	Achieve miracles in life, be at peace	Amethyst Oil of lavender
Third Eye	Raphael	Celestial	Left brain, eyes, pituitary gland	Glaucoma, premature aging, headaches, schizophrenia, dogmatism	Highly intuitive, charismatic, psychic	Blue topaz, lapis Oil – rose geranium

1 Conditions that can be caused by an imbalanced chakra (blocked, low energy or spinning anticlockwise)
2 Chakra is balanced if it is open and spins clockwise

Throat	Michael	Etheric	Thyroid gland, throat, ears, nose	Thyroid problems, sore throats, hearing difficulties	Strong communicator, expressive, easy to meditate	Aquamarine Oil – chamomile
Heart	Chamuel	Astral	Heart, lungs, thymus	Heart problems, cancer, high blood pressure, shallow breathing, feels worthless, fears rejection	Healthy, at ease with oneself, loves easily, compassionate	Rose quartz Oil – rose
Solar plexus	Uriel	Mental	Digestive system, muscles	Weakness, apathy, anger, power games, stomach ulcers	Confidence, self-respect and respect for others, charismatic	Amber, yellow citrine Oil - jasmine

Sacral	Gabriel	Emotional	Ovaries, testes, sex organs, circulatory system	Impotence, frigidity, sexual addition, bladder / prostate / lower back issues	Sexually comfortable, trusting, expressive, creative	Golden topaz Oil –sandalwood
Base / Root	Gabriel	Etheric	Skeletal structure,	Osteoarthritis, difficulty achieving goals, airiness, over materialistic, bullying, aggressive	Grounded, strong physical mastery, achieves results	Bloodstone, garnet Oil – patchouli, musk
Earth Star	Sandalphon	Earth's energy field Deep physical	Deep physical	Inability to connect spiritual to physical or channel light to Earth	Ability to realise full potential, manifestation	Black obsidian Oil – cedar

Figure 2
Aura and
Chakra Interaction -
5th Dimension

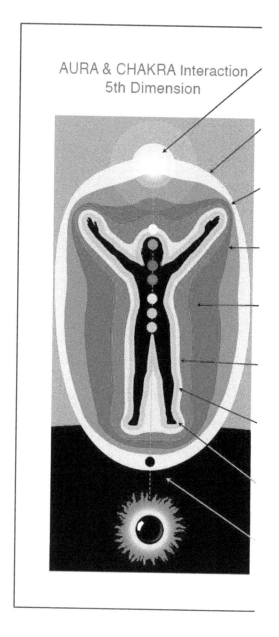

Divine Energy Field *I AM One with the Divine* WHITE	STAR CHAKRA – AA Metatron; related to the Divine energy field; crystals = selenite; if spins anti clockwise emotional condition = megalomania; if open and spinning clockwise pure connection with Source, essential oil = violet
Ketheric Energy Field *I Know the Truth* WHITE VIOLET	CROWN CHAKRA – AA Jophiel; related to ketheric body; crystal = amethyst; linked to right brain and pineal gland, if blocked/unhealthy can lead to Alzheimer's, confusion, paranoia; if open/healthy can achieves miracles in life, at peace, essential oil = lavender
Celestial Energy Field *I AM Integration* LILAC	THIRD EYE CHAKRA – AA Raphael; related to celestial body; crystal = blue topaz, lapis; linked to left brain, eyes, pituitary gland, if blocked/unhealthy linked to glaucoma, premature aging, headaches, schizophrenia, dogmatism; if open highly intuitive, charismatic, psychic; essential oil = rose geranium
Etheric Energy Field *I AM the Voice of Truth* ROYAL BLUE	THROAT CHAKRA – AA Michael; related to etheric template, crystal = aquamarine; linked to thyroid gland, throat, ears, nose; if blocked/unhealthy can lead to thyroid problems, sort throats, hearing difficulties, if open/healthy strong communicator, expressive, easy to meditate; essential oil = chamomile
Astral Energy Field *I AM Unconditional Love* PINK VIOLET	HEART CHAKRA – AA Chamuel; related to astral body; crystal = rose quartz; linked to heart, lungs, thymus; if blocked/unhealthy heart problems, cancer, high blood pressure, shallow breathing, feels worthless, fears rejection; if open/ healthy at ease with oneself, loves easily, compassionate; essential oil: rose
Mental Energy Field *I AM Empowerment* PALE GOLD	SOLAR PLEXUS CHAKRA – AA Uriel; mental body; crystal = amber, yellow citrine; linked to digestive system, muscles; if unhealthy/blocked – weakness, apathy, anger, power games, stomach ulcers; if healthy/open –confident, self respect &for others, charistmatic. Essential oil = jasmine/ grapefruit
Emotional Energy Field *I AM Creation* PEACH	SACRAL CHAKRA – AA Gabriel; crystal = golden topaz; emotional body; linked to ovaries, testes, sex organs, circulatory system, blocked/unhealthy... impotence, frigidity, sexual addiction, bladder/ prostate/lower back issues; open/healthy – sexually comfortable, trusting, expressive, creative. Sandalwood
Etheric Energy Field *I AM Supported* PLATINUM ROSE	BASE CHAKRA – AA Gabriel; crystal = bloodstone/ garnet; etheric body; linked to skeletal structure, problems – osteoarthritis, difficulty achieving goals, airiness, flaky, over materialistic bullying, aggressive; open/healthy = grounded, strong physical mastery, achieves results. Essential oil; patchouli, musk
Earth's Energy Field *I AM One with the Earth* BLACK	EARTH CHAKRA – AA Sandolphon; crystal = black obsidian; deep physical; unopened = inability to connect spiritual to physical or channel light to earth; open = ability to realise full potential & manifest. Essential oil = cedar

Chapter 10

CLEANSING, ENERGISING AND HEALING YOUR CHAKRAS

You can improve the health of your chakras by working at both the physical and energetic / auric levels. Physical approaches include practising yoga, ka huna dancing and massage, bathing with Epson salts or using particular essential oils relating to those chakras, whether in massage, burners or in a bath.

Fresh air, sleep, moderate exercise and good food also improve the health of chakras. Reducing the intake of meat is important to raise your vibrations. Whilst it is still acceptable to eat red and white meat, to develop spiritually it is important that you bless the meat and the Soul of the animal that has passed over. You may also want to consider fasting from meat on certain days.

Reducing toxins and drugs is essential. Hard drugs will limit and sometimes maim your spiritual growth for a lifetime. Drugs like marijuana, alcohol and nicotine have a dulling effect on the senses, which reduces the vibrations and ability to connect to the celestial kingdoms.

Auric approaches to raising one's vibrations include reiki / light-work (only explore with an experienced therapist with whom you resonate), body integration (this realigns the body to its original form and, like ka huna, massage can release trapped emotions and effects of old injuries, even in past lives), visualisations, angel work, psychotherapy / counselling, meditation, self-development, and programming relevant crystals and using them in healing yourselves.

Colour plays a special role in strengthening your chakras – each chakra resonates with particular colours that change as you progress through the dimensions toward enlightenment. Colour can be used in your surroundings, what you wear, the food you eat, or crystals you use to cleanse and strengthen your auras. If you are feeling low on energy in a particular chakra, try adding more of that colour into your life.

Energetic Defence Mechanisms

At a Soul level, when you choose to incarnate on Earth you agree to accept the Veil of Amnesia, which sets Earth apart from most other worlds. In doing so, you forget you are connected to Me, Source; that most of you have had many previous incarnations; and that you will always be supported, protected, loved and nourished.

This is why there is a queue of Souls trying to get a place on Earth – there just aren't many training grounds like it. To wrestle with the Ego, to deal with the physical and sexual challenges of living in an Earthly body, is unlike any other experience.

Fear / anxiety is one of the main challenges you must overcome as humans to reunite yourselves with Me and merge with your Soul / Higher Self and eventually your Monad.

Your Ego is intrinsically insecure and sets up defence mechanisms to deal with its fear. These defence mechanisms manifest in two main ways:

1) Guarding around the body, like armour blocking the flow of energy through the body and the balance of the chakras. This often manifests in particular body shapes including retention of weight in certain areas where the guarding or holding on is taking place. For instance, someone who guards their heart is likely to have slightly hunched shoulders; whereas someone who has a lot of anger may experience a blockage in the flow of energy in the abdomen, and weight retention there.

2) Unhealthy energetic behaviours. You should pay particular attention to how your aura interacts with that of other people around you. The following diagrams illustrate several types of negative interaction.

- In figure 2A the person is an energy vampire, sucking energy from the solar plexus of the other person like an emotional leech. Person 2 will feel depleted and low on energy when they come into contact with person 1.
- In figure 2B the energy field is like a hot spiky presence. Like a porcupine, it is difficult to get close to this person without feeling the jabs. The message is: stay away or else!
- In diagram 2C, 'Hysteria', person 1 is sending energetic stab wounds to the auric field of person 2. These may or may not be accompanied by verbal insults.
- In diagram 2D the person is directing their energy field against themselves, sending negative thoughts like darts into their own energetic field, caused by brooding or self-hate.

Do you recognise any of these energy patterns in yourself? Do you feel depleted, upset or stung in the presence of certain people you know?

A

B

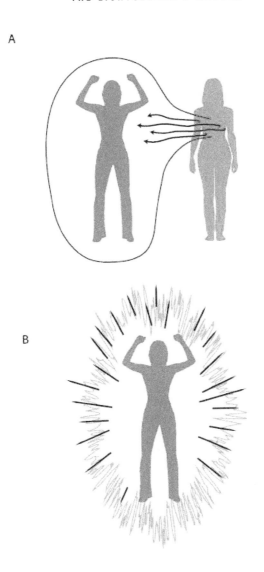

Figure 2

A: Energy vampire sucking the energy from the solar plexus of person 2

B: Porcupine energy field, spiky and difficult to get near

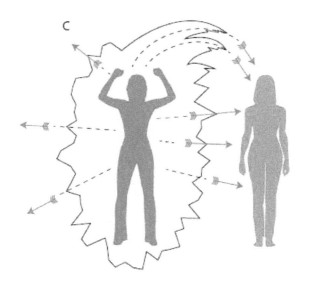

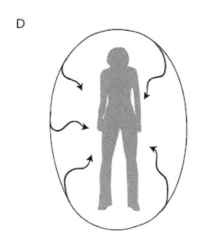

Figure 2

C: Hysteria – Person 1 throws energetic darts at person 2

D: Self-loathing, brooding, attacking oneself

☼ Exercise ☼
To Feel Your Body Armour

Ask the angels to give you hands of light. It may help to visualise your hands surrounded by a beautiful vibrant golden light that heals with touch.

Close your eyes. Either practising on yourself or another person, start with your hands about 60cm from the body and then bring them gradually in toward the body.

Feel different parts of the space around the body. Be aware of where the energy field seems heavy, dense, blocked or stagnant. Ask for healing to be given to that part of the body.

☼ Exercise ☼
To Identify Negative Thought Patterns

Do you have many negative thoughts? Do you think, *Damn, it's raining*, or *I'll never be able to do this or that*, or *I'll never have enough money*, or *I'll never get a partner*, or *I'm bad because I've done this or that.*

Write down all the negative thoughts you have and whether you repeat them. In this way, you will become aware of **your repeating manifestations.** Then you can begin to counteract them.

☼ Exercise ☼
Counteracting the Negatives

Look at all the negative thoughts you have collected. Beside them, write the converse positive. For instance, if you think / say, 'I am guilty of this,' replace it with, 'I am becoming wiser and more loving every day.'

If you say to yourself, 'I'll never have a partner / house / health,' replace it with, 'I have an abundance of love / money / health,' or 'a perfect house / partner / job is coming to me.'

Practise herding your thoughts and focus on what you really want to attract into your life.

☼ Exercise ☼
Focus on Unconditional Love

Become aware of your Ego. The Ego is the part of you that seeks to be superior to others, that wants the bigger house / salary / swimming pool / status because of what other people will think of you. The Ego does not want something for the intrinsic joy such things will give you, irrespective of other people, but is driven by fear and comparisons.

It is not wrong in itself to want material comfort or influence. What is unhealthy and driven by Ego is when your sense of worthiness is dependent upon material possessions or status. Also be aware of the Ego when it says you are better than others because you shun material possessions or because you are more spiritual than others.

The Ego always wants to find a way to be superior. Challenge your motives. Become aware of the Presence behind the Ego. This is the 'I AM' presence that is the essence of you, your connection to your Higher Self (your Soul aspect), your Soul and your Monad.

The biggest source of malady and pain is the lack of love humans have for themselves, and often for others. But it is self-love that will be the biggest aid to healing the body.

Practise shining love to yourself. This is not about Ego. Again, beware of comparing yourself to others and saying you are better. You are no better, but you are amazing – an amazing being created by Me, Source, God, Allah. Therefore, I ask that you embrace your true beauty and shine love on yourself.

Ask Me and I will also shine love, for you are one of My beautiful creations and I have an abundance of love for you.

Every day this week, shine unconditional love on yourself. Imagine the feeling of being in love. Practise this every day. Feel the joy, the utter acceptance of being wholly loved, for all your imperfections, warts and all. Now shine this love out to others around you. Find something to respect in everyone, see through their exterior to their interior – find and love the God-spark in them. You may not like them, but allow your unconditional love to flow.

Ailments and Their Underlying Causes

I will list a number of ailments, the potential underlying reasons for the malady and action that can be taken, including positive affirmations and physical and medicinal responses. It is not comprehensive but gives an indication of where to start. Note that sometimes an illness is there because of a Soul contract and cannot be improved with these actions. However, even in these cases, using positive affirmations, ensuring your chakras are clear and working on the issue as outlined here will assist in your Ascension process. Remember: loving yourself should be the basis of your healing; it all starts and ends with love. Never blame, always love. Also remember that every ailment is an opportunity for growth.

For some of you reading this section, it may seem inappropriate to provide simple words to heal such significant conditions. I say this to you: be aware that in many situations the disease manifests in the auric level before the physical. If you address the root cause at the auric level through energy work, diet, chakra cleansing, working with My angels and dealing with your life issues, many physical problems can be avoided. If the causes suggested in this table do not resonate with you, still your mind and ask your body if there are any negative thought processes influencing your health and healing. Then create positive affirmations that counteract these.

Most of the interventions below are aimed at the auric body, the root cause, as a way of addressing the physical ailment. In some cases conventional medical intervention is the right course of action, to be used in conjunction with auric healing approaches. Listen and follow your intuition, and ask us for guidance.

There will always be illnesses that have been chosen at a Soul contract level. In some instances, these will not be able to be healed by the following direction. However, pursuing this form of healing will help with your rapid Ascension.

Remember the end goal is to reconnect with Me, not necessarily to overcome the condition. This may seem harsh, but the training ground of Earth is a difficult one. It is a training ground that you entered with full awareness of the love and support we in the celestial kingdom have for you. You have incarnated voluntarily. When you return to us through your Ascension you will reconnect to Me, and to our love that flows through everything and everyone. At that point, you will have full awareness once more.

However, part of your ascension process is to try to connect to us, try to understand why you have been given the challenges in your life, and face these challenges with love for yourself.

Table 5 Ailment chart

Ailment	Possible Underlying Cause(s)	Action and Affirmation(s)
Acne	Lack of confidence, self-dislike, lack of physical confidence	Affirmations: 'I am beautiful.' 'God has made me in His / Her image.' 'I lovingly accept myself just as I am.'
AIDS	Severe dislocation from the joy in life, self-hatred and self loathing	Action: Reprogramming of the DNA. This can only be performed by an experienced light-worker. A person can potentially overcome the disease by raising their vibrations to the sixth or seventh dimensions through practices within this book. Affirmations: 'I love myself wholly.' 'Source loves me wholly, for I am created in the perfect form to learn my lessons and Ascend.'
Premature Baldness	Holding on, needing to control everything and everyone	Affirmations: 'I AM flow.' 'I rejoice in others' differences.'
High Blood Pressure	Anxiety, holding on, trying to control every situation, not facing fears, failure to let go	Affirmations: 'I am one with the world.' 'I love myself and others unconditionally.' 'Peace and harmony dwell within me and surround me.'

119

Low Blood Pressure	The minor difficulties of life are a burden, being dragged down by the mundane, failure to see the bigger picture	Action: Tissue salts, yogic breathing, breathing, breath of life, sending love energy to oneself. Affirmation: 'I release the need to hold on. All is well.'
Breast Cancer	Self-hate around body and breasts; inability to nurture oneself	Action: Give praise to oneself, spoil oneself and feel good about it, release guilt about 'not being good enough'; energy work with the heart chakra and Archangels Chamuel (heart chakra) and Raphael (healing). Affirmations: 'I am blessed with a beautiful body.' 'I am an amazing being, beautiful inside and outside.'
Catarrh	Too much, I can't breathe, suffocating, need to get away	Action: Rest and quiet space, work on groundedness, root and throat chakras – need to release negative aura around throat with reiki. Affirmation: 'Rest and peace are here with me.'
Cervical Cancer	Being hard on one-self, on the feminine within; fears of not being a good enough mother / wife / lover / worker	Action: Removal of abnormal cervical tissue called LETTS or LEEP surgical intervention. Affirmations: 'Peace and harmony dwell within me and surround me.' 'I am perfectly created to learn my lessons and Ascend.' 'I am at peace with myself and where I am in my life.'

Colds	Petty difficulties become burdensome, too much going on	Action: Tissue salts and vitamin C, rest and early nights, meditation, relaxing the mind. Affirmation: 'Peace and harmony dwell in me.'
Coughs	Built up anger and resentment; in too much of a hurry	Action: Work on throat chakra with Archangel Michael. Affirmations: 'I love myself and those around me unconditionally.' 'All is well.'
Diarrhoea	Need to release and purge, cleansing, detoxing, need to stop immediately and rest	Action: Bed rest. Affirmation: 'I release all that requires releasing.'
Headache	At odds with the flow of life	Action: Tissue salts for headaches. Affirmation: 'I flow freely with life.'
Lower Back Pains / Frozen Back	Feeling seriously unsupported in life	Action: Energetic alignment through chakra balancing, ignite the Earth star chakra; ask Archangel Gabriel to work with the root and sacral chakras by placing her energy of pink and peach gold energy into those chakras. Affirmations: 'I am one with the Earth.' 'My life flows with the Divine.' 'I am exactly where I am meant to be in my life.'

Prostate Cancer	Lack of self-worth as a man, self-hatred, feeling washed up, fear of taking one's rightful place in the world	Action: Medical, energetic working with root and sacral. Affirmations: 'I am fully supported by the world.' 'I am loved and lovable.' 'I stand in my full power as a man.'
Long-Sightedness	Desire to overcome ones hurdles by focusing on something else, e.g. distraction	Affirmations: 'I lovingly embrace my failings.' 'I am perfect in my imperfection.' 'There is time for everything.'
Short-Sightedness	Failure to see the truth in a situation, failure to face the major issues in one's life	Action: At a physical level, eye exercises to strengthen eye muscles (focus on your thumb in the near ground, then on the horizon, near ground, and horizon – circulate eyes, and rub eyes – yogic exercises). Affirmations: 'I wholly accept my future.' 'I am lovingly ready to face my life lessons.' 'I choose to be my Higher Self.'
Vomiting	Person or place makes one sick	Action: Complete bed rest until the purging is over. Give unconditional love to the person who is irritating or sickening you. Accept that, at a Soul level, there is a lesson you need to learn or a karmic bond that needs working through. This does not mean you have to stay with the person, but release the need to hold on and move on if necessary.

☼☼ Exercise and Visualisation ☼☼
Listening to Your Body

Identify any recurring health issues in your life. Were there any incidents that triggered these episodes?

Relax deeply and ask your body what the root cause of these maladies is. Listen to whatever comes up in the visualisation or over the course of the next few days.

Then take a pen and jot down the affirmations and chakras related to your maladies.

Make time every day to repeat the affirmations that relate to these issues, or ask for angelic guidance as to the affirmations you should use. They should be wholly positive opposites of the underlying cause. If your body / intuition tells you the cause, go with that.

Also focus on the relevant chakra. Send it light and love using the chart in this chapter. Ask to go to the etheric retreat of the Archangel who works with that chakra. You can also ask Archangel Raphael, as she is the angel of healing. Know you can heal yourself – but you must look deeply within and become connected to your body to understand how.

And if you do not heal, know you will be closer to Ascension for trying.

Example Timetable for Weeks 15 and 16

Activity	Week 15							Week 16						
	1	2	3	4	5	6	7	1	2	3	4	5	6	7
Ground and protect yourself every day. Use the Golden Silver Violet flame and the Source or Mahatma Energy every day.	▓	▓	▓	▓	▓	▓	▓	▓	▓	▓	▓	▓	▓	▓
Undertake the exercise to measure your chakras – note which are spinning clockwise or anticlockwise. Work on cleansing and healing the chakras that are out of balance.	▓													
Undertake the exercise to feel your body armour.														
Become aware during the day of how different people and circumstances make you feel. How do they affect your energy field?							▓							
Exercise: Identify negative thought patterns														
Exercise: Counteracting the negatives.			▓											
Exercise: Focus on unconditional love.											▓		▓	
Exercise and Visualisation: Listening to Your Body.														

Chapter 11

UNIVERSAL LAWS

We will not cover all the universal laws, but rather the six laws you need to master in order to Ascend.

These are as follows, and all are imperative, although that of love is the most important:

1. The Law of Unconditional Love – *Unconditional Love Is Happiness*
2. The Law of Manifestation – *Power to Manifest Is Ours*
3. The Law of Attraction
4. The Law of Opposites
5. The Law of Decrees
6. The Power of Now

These are the six laws you must master in order to Ascend.

We have covered this in a previous chapter, so I will not dwell on it here. But in essence, you must understand that to find enlightenment, you must learn to love and accept yourselves just as you are, with all your imperfections – to love yourselves without judgment, whilst at the same time trying to be the best people you can be, trying to become your best and highest selves, merging with your Souls and Monads.

The Law of Unconditional Love also says that love is a flow. There is no limit to the love you may experience, no limit to the love you may receive and no limit on your own love.

The more you love, the more you *can* love; your capacity for love increases until your love reaches not just those immediately close to you, but all of humanity.

This extends to beggars on the street, murderers and rapists. You need not like them, you may severely dislike them, but unconditional love requires that you recognise the God-spark within every living thing.

It also asks you to recognise that whilst an Earthly retribution system is required, at a spiritual level it is not for humans to judge one another. Rather, it is for the Karmic panel I have established as Source to judge the progress and transgressions of a Soul.

To love is the ultimate happiness. Whilst we ask Souls to master unconditional love, when you Ascend to the seventh dimension you will be beings of pure love, able to love without judgment, whatever the transgression, because My energy flows through you and I AM All-Loving.

The Law of Manifestation

The Law of Manifestation is one of the most exciting opportunities for humans to master. Yet it does not apply to material wealth sought through greed or Ego.

Material wealth is not wrong in itself. When you own the ability to manifest, you can create a comfortable lifestyle for your families. But it must be material wealth without Ego. The pursuit of material wealth for the purpose of demonstrating one's superiority will not lead to enlightenment, but to discontent.

So what is the Law of Manifestation? All humans have the ability to reawaken their psychic abilities, to create matter out of nothing. They can draw events, coincidences, relationships, experiences into their lives through positive thought and the understanding that as God flows through each one of them, they have the power to co-create with the Universe.

There are a number of techniques for manifestation. These range from recognising that your negative thoughts need to be herded into well-ordered, positive thoughts to drawing visual posters that illustrate the things you want to manifest.

If you have not manifested something you want, it may be for two reasons: 1) it is not the right time for you to manifest – there is a lesson you need to learn before manifesting this particular thing, or 2) it is not in your best interests. It may also be because you are not applying your whole attention, using all your physical sensations to manifest.

The Law of Attraction

The Law of Attraction is closely linked to the Law of Manifestation. Here you recognise that if you behave in a certain way, you will attract what you give out. If you give out negative thoughts and perform destructive deeds, if you are greedy, judgmental, needy, then you will attract aspects of these actions. You will be surrounded by negative energy.

If you are diligent in the thoughts you think, replacing negative thoughts with positive ones – if you do good deeds for others, live consciously with the planet, and generally live higher, loving lives – then you will attract into your lives an abundance of good things, loving relationships, positive experiences and kind deeds in return.

Don't get caught out by thinking that living a life with positive thoughts and deeds will mean you cease to experience any challenging events. You may all have heard about a particularly good person who has succumbed to cancer. This is not caused by the Law of Attraction, but the result of a Soul contract that needs to be played out and could not have been avoided. Also, just because a miser is rich, this does not mean the Law of Attraction is not at work. There are a number of factors that dictate the experiences of a person; one is the Law of Attraction, but karma and Soul contracts are other factors.

However, in general, the more positive you are, the more positivity you will attract and vice versa.

The Law of Opposites

The Law of Opposites is just as it sounds: if you send a message to the Universe that you are white, the Universe will respond by becoming blacker.

This does not mean the Universe creates more darkness when you become light, but rather the brighter your light shines, the darker that around you may seem.

What is happening is the vibrations of the whole world are rising, as is the average level of light at work. Do not be caught out by thinking that if you a bad deed, somewhere else there will be light – but the Law of Karma does require balance.

So if you commit a bad deed, it will require cancellation. The Law of Karma is integrally linked with the Law of Opposites; you will always have to pay for your deeds.

The Law of Decree

When you reach the seventh dimension, you recognise your intrinsic ability to co-create with the Universe. This is the point when you know My energy flows through you; you have reconnected to Me. A decree is when you order the universe to reposition itself to bring about a certain event or outcome.

By repeating three times your chosen decree, the Universe reconvenes to your command. Be aware that by the time you reach the seventh dimension, you have committed your life in service to the Divine, so decrees will not be self-seeking but for your good, and that of the world and the Universe.

When using decrees before the Veil of Amnesia has been lifted, you must be accurate in what you are decreeing.

You may decree to release all your issues and to learn all your lessons to Ascend; this may result in a host of major life challenges being brought forward.

So be aware of what you are decreeing, and that the consequences may not be obvious. To 'decree', always use a sentence construction as follows:

'I decree under the grace of God that ....
...... So be it, it is done.' Repeat this three times. This ensures all decrees are done for your highest benefit (under the Grace of God).

The Power of Now

You expend so much energy worrying about past decisions or other paths you could have taken, as well as future events that may or may not come to pass.

The Law of the Power of Now is recognising the full power you have to act over this instant; and by being present in the Now, you maximise your own energy use. You also allow the magic of the moment to seize you; you see with new, clear eyes.

It is the strength of acting now, when multiplied a million fold by all the choices made in each moment, that will allow you to operate at full perception and strength and will enable **any** path to be followed, however challenging it may seem.

Exercises to Bring the Seven Laws into Your lives

☼ Exercise & Visualisation ☼
Bringing in Unconditional and Pure Love

Write a list of all the times you have failed to live up to your own expectations. Why did you feel you hadn't achieved what you 'should' have?

Write down which of these feelings you can trace back to when you were a child. Were your parents or influential adults particularly hard on you or did you feel rejected by them in some way? Did you feel they loved you more if you behaved a certain way? Did a certain event impact you in a major way?

Now close your eyes and imagine you are sitting on a white cloud in Heaven. Beside you sits your Guardian Angel. They give you a beautiful, pure pale pink flower, but as soon as you take it, it withers.

Your Guardian Angel tells you this is *You*, and that together, you need to revive the flower so you can be healthy and feel loved. Tears come to your eyes at how lonely and vulnerable you feel.

From a bag, your Guardian Angel removes a cup and a flask, both made of gold. Into the cup, they pour a liquid from the flask.

You take the cup and drink the liquid. It tastes deliciously sweet, the most amazing drink you've ever tasted. The cup never gets empty. When you have drunk your fill, the cup is still brimming with this amazing liquid. This is the cup of abundance, and it is yours to keep with you at all times.

Now your Guardian Angel dips the cup into his or her chest and fills it with pure love. Pure love is made of the Source Energy that is in every living thing.

Your Guardian Angel now asks you to recline on the cloud, which is comfortable. Your Guardian Angel pours the pure love into your heart chakra. They pour and pour and pour and pour, until the pure love flows out of your heart chakra because it is so full.

When you sit up again, you feel your heart pulsing with love and happiness. You feel your whole body tingling with vitality. You feel completely connected to Me, to the angelic kingdom, and to every living thing in the Earth. This is what it feels like to live in the seventh dimension.

When you are ready, open your eyes. Notice the difference in the colours around you, and in how you see people and objects.

⊙ Visualisation⊙
With Archangel Zadkiel on Forgiveness

Breathe deeply and evenly. Feel your feet firmly on the floor. Tiny golden roots grow down from the soles of your feet into the beautiful magical African soil, down, down, down until they reach a magnificent black obsidian crystal at the centre of the Earth.

The tiny golden roots wrap themselves around the crystal and you breathe in the energy from the crystal, up, up, up into your body. When you breathe out, tiny multi-coloured stars come out through the top of your head and fall down the sides of your body, protecting and grounding you on the Earth.

Ask Archangel Michael to encircle you in a bubble of his blue light of protection and post an angel of protection above you, one below you, one to the left and one to the right of you, one before and one behind you.

Now ask Archangel Chamuel to encircle you in a large ball of brilliant rose-white light, the light of pure love. You are completely grounded and protected.

You stand in a safe, calming room. In the room are two comfortable chairs. Look around you and take in your surroundings.

Beside you appears your Guardian Angel. Feel the love your Guardian Angel feels for you, pure unconditional love. You can feel it radiate from your Guardian Angel and it makes you feel safe, nurtured and truly loved and valued.

Greet your Guardian Angel. If you haven't met your Guardian Angel before, ask them their name and thank them for being here with you today, and for always being with you, for they have accompanied you in every lifetime.

In the centre of the room is a fountain of Golden Silver Violet flames. You feel the presence of the mighty Archangel Zadkiel, who is the guardian of the Golden Silver Violet flame. She is here to help you forgive and be forgiven.

She asks you to know deeply that the sufferings you have experienced serve to enable your spiritual development, and that you have made Soul contracts with these Souls for you both to learn the necessary lessons to progress.

She understands that forgiveness can be difficult, but she and your Guardian Angel are with you to help.

Your Guardian Angel now asks you to sit in one of the two chairs. They wrap their wings around you and take you to sit on one of the comfortable chairs.

Your Guardian Angel then walks across the room to a door in the wall opposite you. They are going to invite someone from whom you need to **receive** forgiveness.

Your Guardian Angel opens the door under the loving gaze of Archangel Zadkiel. Someone whose forgiveness you require now enters the room.

Your Guardian Angel walks them to the chair opposite you and the person sits down. You greet the person with unconditional love and they greet you with unconditional love.

Archangel Zadkiel now envelops you in the Golden Silver Violet flame. It dances around you and the person sitting opposite you, transmuting any negativity you may feel to positivity. Feel it dissolve all negativity. It feels good.

Now the Golden Silver Violet flame recedes and you feel lighter. Listen to what the person sitting opposite you has to say. If you want to say anything, do so.

Hear them forgive you for what you have done to them in this or a past life.

Thank the person for their forgiveness, and watch as your Guardian Angel accompanies them across the room and out the door.

Your Guardian Angel now invites someone who has **hurt you** in this or a past life, whom **you are ready to forgive**.

Your Guardian Angel returns with this person. They walk across the room and this person sits down opposite you. Greet the person with unconditional love and receive their greeting of unconditional love.

Once again, Archangel Zadkiel surrounds you in the Golden Silver Violet flame.

Feel any negativity in your body, mind or aura turn to positivity.

Listen as the person asks your forgiveness. Know deeply that you have a Soul contract with them and the hurt they have caused you is part of this contract.

When you are ready, give them your forgiveness. Forgiving them makes you feel lighter. Thank them and watch as your Guardian Angel walks them out of the room.

Your Guardian Angel has now gone to fetch your Higher Self.

Into the room walks a shining beautiful You, your Higher Self.

Greet your Higher Self with unconditional love and receive their greeting of unconditional love. Your Higher Self sits down opposite you.

This is your time to forgive yourself for all the hurt you have caused yourself or hurt you have caused others, including all the times you were too hard on yourself.

Your Higher Self listens intently, and then tells you how lovable you are; you are an amazing being who is valuable, loveable and beautiful.

Receive this blessing from your Higher Self. Archangel Zadkiel now surrounds you in the Golden Silver Violet flame of transmutation.

You feel the negativity slip away, replaced by positivity.

You forgive yourself totally and recognise the essential beauty and goodness that dwells within you. You are designed to be exactly as you are meant to be in this life, at exactly the right stage of spiritual development for this life, at exactly the right point in every aspect of your life.

Completely accept yourself, just as Archangel Zadkiel, your Guardian Angel and your Higher Self do.

Thank your Higher Self and watch as your Guardian Angel accompanies your Higher Self out of the room.

Your Guardian Angel returns to the room and sits opposite you. Your Guardian Angel now gives you a message.

Thank your Guardian Angel for the message. Thank Archangel Zadkiel for the Golden Silver Violet flame and know that you can use it any time of day, as many times as you need it. Archangel Zadkiel is always there for you and you feel her love.

You say goodbye and return to this room. Feel your feet on the ground and become aware of your breathing. Rub your fingers and thumbs together.

☼ Visualisation ☼
On the Law of Manifestation

Sit quietly and close your eyes. Ground and protect yourself.

You are suspended in space. Around you, the stars twinkle. You are weightless, yet held securely. You feel stable and complete.

Open your arms to welcome the blessings the Universe has to shine on you.

Become aware of something you truly desire – not for your Ego, but for your true love of yourself and the world.

With each breath, breathe pink-gold love energy into the image of what you would like. Imagine what you want suspended before your eyes. Soon, the image of what you truly desire is filled and surrounded by this love energy.

Now become aware of the Universe moving around you. Slowly and gradually, the Universe moves to a new position, bringing your true desire to you.

You feel a rush of warm gold energy flood through your heart chakra and through the rest of your body. This is pure joy, connecting with the joy of the Universe. Know with deep certainty that you have manifested what you truly want.

Place a time on when you will manifest it in the physical; it may be a day, a week, a year. Whatever the timeframe, know it will come to you at the right time, because you are a co-creator with the Universe and with Source.

☼⟐ Exercise and Visualisation⟐ ☼
For the Law of Attraction

Write down the key events in your life along a timeline, starting from when you were born until now. Write down the emotions you felt at each time. If there were periods in your life when you felt a particular emotion, write this down on the timeline

Now see if there are any repeating patterns. Was there more than one event or time in your life when you felt rejected, or a failure, or victimised, or joyful, happy, loved?

Recognise the parts of yourself that hold some of these emotions. Own these *parts* of you, but know *they are not you*; they are lessons to be overcome or learnt.

If you have experienced much rejection, become aware of the parts of you that reject yourself, that judge yourself as not being worthy or good enough.

If there were times when you were happy and carefree, become aware of how you felt about yourself at those points. Were you more loving or nurturing toward yourself?

You experience externally what you create internally. It is now time to change your inner environment.

Close your eyes and ground and protect yourself. Find yourself standing on a riverbank. The sun is shining and the temperature is perfect.

It is the river of expectation. This river has always been un-crossable. But now you are ready to cross to the other side.

How can you cross? The river is deep and there is no boat.

You imagine yourself on the other side of the water. But that person is also stuck. Now you realise that to get to the other side, you have to be all the best parts of yourself at the same time.

Watch yourself on the other bank and wave. Feel joyful and loving toward yourself. That You is mighty and invincible. Watch as your Self walks toward you, across the deep, swiftly flowing water.

This image of you does not falter, but continues to look you straight in the eye. Feel the strength and beauty of your Self: the goodness, the honesty, the love for everything.

For this is the River of Truth. If you are not your highest Self, you will sink, but if you stand as your best and highest Self, you can walk across the water.

When you look down, you realise you have crossed to the centre of the river. You have met your Self, your beautiful strong Self.

You raise your hand and touch your hand to your mirror image. As you do so, the river beneath you disappears and instead you stand before Jesus Christ, who holds the Christ Consciousness energy.

Jesus places the Christ Consciousness Energy in your heart chakra, thanks you and kisses your forehead.

Next you find standing before you Prophet Mohammed; he gives you the gift of the energy of Divine wisdom and places it in your third eye. He thanks you, kisses your forehead and disappears.

Now before you appears the Buddha, who gives you the energy of joy and security, and places it in your sacral and base chakras.

Finally, before you stands Ray o' Light. He gives you the energy of fearlessness and places it in your solar plexus.

You feel your body pulse with love, joy, wisdom, invincibility, humility and security.

When you are ready, open your eyes and return to the physical world, knowing that you are your highest Self.

☼ Exercise ☼
For the Law of Opposites

This is the exercise on the Law of Opposites. Mastering this law is one of the biggest challenges. Humans like to think they are unable to lie, but you lie to yourselves all the time.

The Law of Opposites dictates that you have complete honesty within yourselves, about your deepest wishes and fears.

I want you to start by writing a list of your innermost fears, however private and deeply hidden. These may seem small and trivial, but write them all down.

Now look at what the opposites would be. Look at what your life would be like if the perfect opposite, the perfect balance were introduced to counteract these fears.

This is the balance you need to introduce. If you fear losing your home, counteract it with the joy of feeling secure in your home. If you fear being without money, think about an abundance of financial wealth in your life and how it would feel. If you fear being alone, feel the opposite – what it would be like to be in a harmonious relationship.

If you fear dependency on another, feel the emancipation of always being content with your own company.

Whatever the fear, accept it now and become aware that within you there is perfect balance, and that both forces co-exist.

Now you must increase the force within yourself of the opposite of what you fear. To do this, we will undertake a visualisation.

❂ Visualisation ❂
On the Law of Opposites

Relax and feel your feet on the magical soil of the Earth. Ask for protection and ground yourself.

You find yourself in a constellation, in outer space. Around you is perfect blackness, dotted with bright stars powered by pure love.

You bring the first fear to your attention. It floats in front of you like a dark green globe of light. Toward this dark green globe now comes an equally bright light of gold. The two globes of light float in front of you, in perfect balance.

Now the gold light begins to shine more brightly. It is the opposite of your fear. It is the knowledge that you will always be safe and loved.

This light becomes so bright that it swallows you and you find yourself standing fully within its brightness. Feel the abundance, the security and the joy.

With each fear, imagine the dark green globe floating before you and then the bright gold globe that joins it, initially even and balanced and then growing in light until they fully consume you. This is the Law of Opposites: to understand that all fears have an opposite that lies within you, and that you can shine out the fear and move into My Light.

I bless you. Welcome to the mastery of the Law of Opposites.

☼ Exercise ☼
For the Law of Decree

The Law of Decree is very powerful. An important part of its power lies in belief in your ability to co-create with the Universe. There are three decrees that I would like you to undertake, if you are ready. The first is to release all karmic debt.

To prepare for the decree, imagine how you would feel if you were all the highest parts of yourself, the best parts of you. Stand with your shoulders back, head up, legs slightly apart. Imagine white light flooding through you, cleansing you, relaxing you. Feel humble in the light of the Divine that shines through and all around you. When you are ready, speak out loud the following decrees:

I Decree, under the Grace of God, that all karmic debt I have inherited in this life from my previous incarnations, or additional karmic debt I have acquired in this lifetime, I now fully release with love and light, knowing that I stand in my full power as an Ascended Master. So be it, it is done. [Repeat three times]

I Decree, under the Grace of God, that all negative attachments in this or previous lives, I now release fully and forever. So be it, it is done. [Repeat three times]

I Decree, under the Grace of God, that I commit my life to my best and highest path, and the best and highest paths of the planet Earth and the Universe. I do this in love, light and humility. So be it, it is done. [Repeat three times]

☼ Exercise ☼
For the Power of Now

Sit comfortably on a chair or cross-legged on the floor. Feel connected to the Earth; become aware of your breathing. Breathe in for four beats, hold for four beats, again and again.

Concentrate on your breathing, emptying your mind of all other things. With each exhalation, relax a little more, become a part of the Earth a little more.

Allow your mind to float in empty space, like a feather held still on the air. If the feather floats, accept where it floats, but do not focus on anything or any thought that swims into your mind.

Relax, continue to focus on your breathing and just let your mind, the feather, hang suspended in the air, or float.

Be aware that you are within the Now.

☼ Exercise ☼
Releasing Limiting Beliefs

The purpose of this exercise is to become aware of issues or events in your life that you have not let go of, or future events you are anxious about, which are limiting your ability to stand in the Now.

Write down any past regrets, major or minor. Have you regretted not accepting a particular job or going out with a particular person?

Have you regretted becoming involved with a particular person or moving to a certain house or place?

Write down all the regrets you have. Regrets are usually attached to assuming that if you had made a different decision, life would be better than it is now.

Now write down anything you are worried might or might not happen in the future. It could be to do with yourself, your children, your partner, or a work situation. What is preoccupying your mind? What keeps you from sleeping?

◈ Visualisation ◈
To Release Past and Future Anxieties

Ground and protect yourself. Find yourself sitting in the middle of a golden bridge. On one side of the bridge is your past.

See lined up symbols or images of all the events, people and opportunities you regret taking or not taking.

Cross to this side of the bridge and greet or acknowledge each of these regrets (the people, the symbols representing a particular choice you made). Understand the lesson you needed to learn by experiencing what you did.

You may be given a gift by some of the people who represent the choices you have made. Give them your thanks and cross back to the centre of the golden bridge.

Now it is time to face your future anxieties. Walk to the side of the bridge you have not yet visited.

Here are all the people, issues and challenges you are worried about. Greet each and ask them to explain the lesson you need to learn.

They may also give you a gift or something that represents the lesson of your concern. Thank them and cross back to the centre of the bridge.

You are holding a number of gifts and insights from the past and the future. God now surrounds you, and you are transcended by the beauty and goodness of the Power that is Everything and All Things.

Before you is a golden pot. Place all these thoughts and gifts into the golden pot. God now lifts the golden pot and surrounds it with golden loving light.

Then, as you watch it lift above your head, it evaporates into a thousand golden doves that fly away.

You are left in the centre of the bridge, but now realise that below you is the most magnificent river.

You have the power to step onto the river and experience the River of Life in each magnificent moment, with God within and around you.

Feel the power of the Now. Feel the power of God within you.

Example Timetable for Weeks 19 and 20

Activity	Week 19							Week 20						
	1	2	3	4	5	6	7	1	2	3	4	5	6	7
Ground and protect yourself every day.	X												X	X
Use the Golden Silver Violet flame and the Source or Mahatma Energy every day.	X												X	X
Visualisation with Archangel Zadkiel on Forgiveness.														
Visualisation on the Law of Manifestation.			X											
Exercise and Visualisation for the Law of Attraction.					X									
Exercise for the Law of Opposites.								X						
Visualisation on the Law of Opposites.								X						
Exercise for the Law of Decree.										X				
Exercise for the Power of Now.												X		
Exercise for Releasing Limiting Beliefs.														X
Visualisation to Release Past and Future Anxieties.														

Chapter 12

THE WORLD'S ASCENSION

Now is an incredibly important time for the Earth. As I have said, Earth hangs in the balance.

It is up to you to decide whether you are willing to put the time, effort and love into raising your vibrations, which in turn will raise the vibrations of the world.

There are a number of steps that must be taken for the world to Ascend. The first, on which you have already begun working, is to cleanse, heal and energise your chakras by undertaking the visualisations and exercises in this Manual necessary to raise your own vibrations, which will increase the light you emanate.

This light will ripple out like sunbeams into the shadows of the world and make the world a brighter, more amazing place to live.

The second thing that needs to be done is for you to beam out your light and love to the world *consciously*, with particular focus on places troubled by conflict, greed, war, poverty and desperation coming from oppression and unequal rights between the sexes.

The third thing that must be done is for the great portals of the world to be opened. At the same time, they must be cleansed and healed.

I have sent the Channel writing this book to the Earth with the express purpose of working on the cosmic portals. She works closely with other beings of light.

There are also other light-workers in different parts of the world playing an essential role in opening and cleansing the portals at sea and the smaller portals, as well as those who will be able to focus on opening the gateways at the appropriate time.

I want you all to start opening, cleansing and healing portals. This is of the utmost importance to the world's chakras and Ascension.

The World's Chakras

The world has chakras, just like humans do. They are centres of energy in the Earth that need to be in balance and open for the world to be healthy.

The vibrations of these chakras need to be raised so the Earth can Ascend. Table 6 shows the 13 chakras of the world, their location, the issue with which they resonate, and the Archangel and Ascended Master attuned to that chakra.

To heal and balance the Earth's chakras, first you have to cleanse your own chakras, thereby raising your own vibrations.

Whilst I have given a dispensation for those reading My Manual to work on only nine personal chakras, in order for the Earth to Ascend, you must work on its full range of thirteen chakras. In this Manual, the star chakras in the human exercises apply to the stellar gateway, causal and Soul star chakras of the world. The sacral chakra in the exercises for humans applies to the sacral and naval chakras of the world.

Table 6 The World's Chakras and Celestial Guardians

World Chakras	Location	Particular Issue	Archangel and *Ascended Master*
Stellar Gateway	Arctic	Enlightenment	Metatron All Masters work as this bridge from the Divine
Soul Star	Agra, India	Cleansing of old issues (baggage)	Mariel *Rakowski, Isis*
Causal	Tibet	Accessing Divine wisdom	Christiel *Lao Tze*
Crown	Machu Picchu, Peru	Human spirituality and upliftment, bridging the physical and etheric	Jophiel *Mother Mary*
Third Eye	Afghanistan	Power of desire, manifestation for the good of humankind and the world	Raphael *Goddess of Liberty*

Throat	Luxor, Egypt	Speaking the truth, emancipation of the world's peoples, animal and plant kingdoms	Michael

Serapis Bey |
| Cosmic Heart | Guatemala | The centre of the Universe, transcending greed to own self-love and pure love | Butalyl

Jesus |
| Heart | Glastonbury, UK | The heart of the world, pure love, unconditional on race, gender, history or species | Chamuel

Mary Magdalene |
| Solar Plexus | South Africa | Power for the good of humanity, fearlessness | Uriel

Ray o' Light |
| Naval | Fiji | Sexual fulfilment and contentment, respecting the universal sanctity of marriage | Gabriel

Aphrodite |
| Sacral | Honolulu | Creativity, abundance and harmony between the sexes | Gabriel

St Germain |

Root	Gobi Desert, China	Pivotal survival, safety, security, passion, vitality	Gabriel *Prophet Mohammed*
Earth Star	London, UK	Fulfilling the total potential of the world as an Ascended planet with all living in the fifth dimension or above	Sandalphon *Lady Gaia*

The World's Cosmic Portals

We must also open the great cosmic portals of Earth – doorways in the Earth's aura. There are 99 major cosmic portals in the Earth. If these are opened, great influxes of Divine energy and information can flow through them – enough to raise the world to a higher trajectory.

The opening of portals will allow negative energy trapped in the Earth's aura to leave, further raising the vibrations. Souls trapped in the world between life and the afterlife can also easily move through the portals if requested by the opener of the portal.

To open a portal, a light-worker has to be physically beneath the portal, unless they have mastered the powers of their light-bodies.

They must then apply to the celestial kingdom for the portal to be cleansed and opened.

The Source Energy or the Mahatma Energy will always be needed to open a portal. The light-worker must allow the energy to flow through their body and aura, into the Earth.

The first portal was opened in Egypt on the 11th day of the 11th month, 2011. 40-50 portals had to be cleansed and opened by the end of 2013 for the Earth to be on track for Ascension. This took place.

The World's Cosmic Gateways

The cosmic gateways are entry and exit points for moving through the Earth's aura at great distances and great speeds. It is not yet possible to use them, but when the portals are open, with the new level of psychic knowledge that will be endowed to the inhabitants of the planet as their vibrations rise, this future mode of travel will become a reality.

Music is particularly important to opening these gateways. Do not underestimate the power of great music, in particular that of Bach and Beethoven, which chimes with a particularly powerful harmonic convergence.

The Significance of 11/11/11

11/11/11 was a significant time because humans decided it should be significant. 11/11/11 at 11am signalled the time in this era for the opening of the first cosmic portal on Earth.

This was the great portal at the Luxor Temple in Egypt. This great cosmic portal had lain dormant for 100,000 years. It was opened by the Channel and the Principle of the Angel Connection School, and many from the Angel Connection School and Diana Cooper School held the light.

It was particularly important that other light-workers attended the Sphinx and the Great Giza pyramid at this same time. This enabled the completion of the Sacred Triangle between the Luxor Temple, the Sphinx and the Giza pyramid – see figure 3, which illustrates the diary of light-work running up to and including 11/11/11 and the Sacred Triangle.

Throughout the world, other light-workers held the light of this magical time. It was their light and love for the world and humanity that enabled the Divine information to be brought through the now opened portal.

Serapis Bey has his etheric retreat over the Temple of Luxor. He worked closely with the Channel and Principle to open the portal. He gave his messages through channelling via the Principle, and these should be read and understood by all.

11th November 2011, Channelling of Serapis Bey at the Luxor Temple, by Margi McAlpine, Principle of the Angel Connection School of Africa

I am Serapis, come forth from Spirit. Greetings.

The date of the 11th of the 11th 2011 originally had no special significance, but as humankind as a collective human consciousness decided this would be an auspicious day, so it became one.

There is an alignment of certain planets today and a softening of the feminine energy of the full moon. 11 is important, for you stand at the 11th hour. It is as you have been told. The balance of the world is on the 11th hour. What is of great importance is understanding the raising of your vibrations.

In times gone by, man functioned in the fifth dimension and, after the fall, went right back to the third dimension. Some years ago, there was a shift back to the fourth dimension, and yet you need to understand there is a split between the third and fourth dimensions and between the fourth and fifth dimensions, in that you go up and down between the third and fourth until you have fully, consciously made up your mind to move into the fourth.

The same applies when you go between the fourth and fifth dimensions. As you move from the third to the fourth dimension, you become aware of your heart chakra, which needs to be opened.

What happens when you move between the fourth and fifth dimensions is an understanding of the Christ Consciousness Energy, which needs to come into an open heart chakra. It is only by the raising of the vibrations that those Masters who slumber will now awaken.

Every decision is a conscious one; nothing is by chance. Time is of the essence. We have repeated this over and over again and you need to understand this.

The triangle of energy you were made aware of between the Temple of Luxor, the Great Pyramid and the Sphinx is of huge importance, for it is in this area that much of the information is held.

It is this information that will allow you to Ascend. Go back to your ancientness and your wisdom, for each and every one of you is an Ancient Being.

Please understand the seriousness of this. There is no longer time to make decisions that are not absolutely perfect and correct for you.

It is now possible for all other portals to be opened. Not until the great Luxor portal was opened could the other cosmic portals be opened.

It is significant that the Luxor portal is the first because Luxor is also the throat chakra of the world. The throat signifies communication of Divine wisdom.

I rained down Divine information through the Luxor portal, through the light-workers in the temple and into the ground.

They then took the information energetically and physically to the Sphinx and Giza pyramid. In sacred ceremonies, they grounded the information, and then pushed the information through the Earth's energy lines so the information is now accessible to humankind.

What is now necessary is that the remaining portals be opened so we can send down an abundance of energy and information.

What, I hear you ask, is the nature of the information we will provide to you? It is information of technologies you can use to better your own standard of living, whilst protecting the planet. It is information about raising your vibrations. It is energies that will cleanse and heal the toxins of the planet, so the Earth herself can raise her vibrations and Ascend.

It is advanced information about transport modalities that do not require dirty fuel. It is information about levitation and teleportation, and contact with other life forms that want to work with you for peace and love.

It is information about how you can heal diseases and rejuvenate yourselves so you need not fall sick.

All of this information we will send down as the portals open. It is for you all to open these portals, which is one of the main purposes of this Manual.

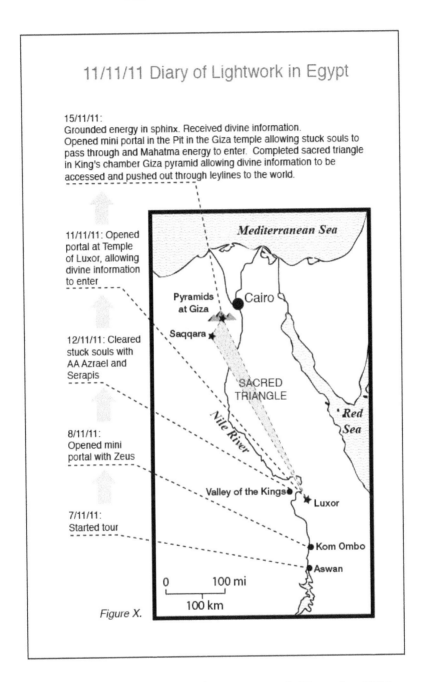

11/11/11 Diary of Lightwork in Egypt

15/11/11:
Grounded energy in sphinx. Received divine information.
Opened mini portal in the Pit in the Giza temple allowing stuck souls to
pass through and Mahatma energy to enter. Completed sacred triangle
in King's chamber Giza pyramid allowing divine information to be
accessed and pushed out through leylines to the world.

11/11/11: Opened
portal at Temple
of Luxor, allowing
divine information
to enter

Mediterranean Sea

Pyramids
at Giza

Cairo

Saqqara

12/11/11: Cleared
stuck souls with
AA Azrael and
Serapis

SACRED
TRIANGLE

Red
Sea

Nile River

8/11/11:
Opened mini
portal with Zeus

7/11/11:
Started tour

Valley of the Kings

Luxor

Kom Ombo

Aswan

0   100 mi

100 km

Figure X.

Figure 3 Diary of Light-work in Egypt 11th November 2011

151

Egypt – The Throat Chakra

Egypt is incredibly important for the Earth's development. Hosting the throat chakra, it will have particular issues surrounding communication and allowing people to speak their truth.

The country has gone off track and the leaders are no longer great. This must change and, with the opening of the portal and the run-up to 11/11/11, this change has already started happening.

United Kingdom – Earth Star and Heart Chakras

There is much I wish to tell you of other countries. Let's start with the United Kingdom, where we have two important chakras. The UK hosts the Earth star and heart chakras.

Both are extremely powerful chakras. Issues concerning groundedness and bringing wisdom of the Universe into the Earth are significant in London.

London had much power at one time, power that it did not use for total good. It will now have another chance for great global influence, but in a positive direction.

It must harness the wisdom of its people, particularly in the area of green technologies and policies and the politics that go with this. Britain remains influential in the world, and in the European Union. It must use this influence for good.

The heart is often the most difficult chakra for humans to balance in their own bodies. We protect the heart by sealing it with layers of protection or, alternatively, by stopping the flow of energy through the chakra altogether.

Similarly, the heart chakra in the UK is a challenging chakra to balance, but as the people of the world open their hearts, so the heart chakra of the world will be cleansed and the vibrations will rise.

There is also a great portal above the heart chakra and once this is opened, Divine love from the celestial kingdom will flow freely into the heart chakra. This portal must be opened soon.

It is not by coincidence that the Olympics took place in London, the position of the Earth star chakra, in the year 2012. It was incredibly important to have this *flushing* through the world of good feeling, joy and exhilaration that the Olympics and Paralympics brought. *Love energy* flooded the Earth, and the energies shared throughout the world, during the games, held the energy of the world at a very high vibration, which has helped significantly in raising the Earth's vibrations.

It was important that the portal above London was opened before the Olympics began. This was done by the Channel and a fellow light-worker. It was essential that the male and female energies of the Earth star chakra were balanced. For many years, across centuries, the energies in London have been male-dominated, full of superiority and guilt.

Bringing the Divine female into London and into the Earth star chakra, by opening the portal above it, was part of the preparation for the world to be on track for the Golden Age, starting with the great shift in 2012.

Do not think this has been predetermined, and do not think Ascension is now inevitable. But these events – the opening of the great cosmic portal, balancing of the Earth star chakra and then the raising of the vibrations through the Olympics and Paralympics – have all enabled the Earth to shift to a higher trajectory. By *trajectory* we mean a higher potential evolved state of the world. I ask you to keep expanding your own love and light, reader of My Manual, and you will enable the Golden Age.

Stellar Gateway – Arctic

The Arctic is threatened. It has been the place of purity for many thousands of years, yet now humans threaten it with their greed and destruction of the planet. It must be protected and saved. Keeping the stellar gateway cleansed and pure is essential for the planet to Ascend. Once it is compromised, it will make it more difficult for the Earth to Ascend, although not impossible. Time is of the essence. A major cosmic portal exists here, near to the chakra. Once this portal is opened, the chakra will have more protection.

Honolulu – Sacral

Hawaii, what a beautiful place. One of My finest creations. The whole of the Pacific represents the sensuality of the senses, to touch, taste, hear, see. All the senses are activated in the Pacific.

Hawaii retains its sacred path, despite being compromised by settlers driven by greed. The original Ka Hunas, although limited in number, still maintain the balance of the island.

The chakra is safe, but needs to be brought to a healthier balance. Sensuality can become indulgent and excessive. Guard against this by investing in the island's sacred places.

The portal in Honolulu must be opened, to enable the chakra to be brought into balance.

Guatemala – Cosmic Heart

The cosmic heart is the heart of the Universe, rather than the heart of the planet Earth. So in addition to the heart of the Earth, we have the heart of the whole Universe here.

This is an incredible blessing, but also a responsibility. What does it mean to be the cosmic heart? It means that the Earth was chosen to be the Universe's centre of love.

This means that if the Earth is out of balance, the whole Universe will be out of balance. The Mayans protected the heart for many centuries, recognising the sacredness of what they had to protect, although not understanding the meaning.

They also compromised it, for although they inherited elements of wisdom from earlier influential civilisations, they were blocked in their own heart chakras.

Now you see why the Earth is so important to us, for it influences the progression of the whole Universe. Until recently, the cosmic heart of the world was blocked. Fortunately, the Channel, working with another light-worker, has cleansed and partially opened it. But it will require further light-work and healing by you all for it to be fully opened and healed.

Once the cosmic heart is in balance, the whole Universe will be in balance. This is possible within your generation, if you begin work on yourselves, loving yourself and others, unconditionally and purely.

Whilst the world continues to hang in balance, the impending disaster predicted at the end of 2012 has been deferred indefinitely; but it is critically dependent upon what you, My beloveds, do from now on. I cannot stomach the exploitation of the planet that you are wreaking, the war and greed that many of the population of Earth leave as their legacy in what is one of the Universe's most beautiful arenas.

I ask you to change your approach to the world. Beam your love out like a lighthouse. Know that by creating ripples of love and honour of the planet, you will change the behaviour of those around you. In this way, you will enable the opening of the cosmic heart to its full glory and bring in the Golden Age.

Machu Picchu, Peru – Crown

A mighty place. A deeply sacred and spiritual place that has not lost its energy, despite the absence of protectors for many centuries. This is where one of the great crystals of the Earth is located, deep within the ground.

This crystal has maintained the balance of this chakra, and it remains protected and hidden from humans with lower motivations.

Much of the world's current Divine information is stored beneath Machu Picchu and much more will flow through Machu Picchu.

Whilst 40-50 portals required opening by the end of 2013, some portals needed opening more quickly. The Earth star and crown are two of these.

The cosmic portal above the crown chakra was opened in 2013, just in time. The light-workers who opened it continue to hold it in the light, but more people need to shine their light to the chakra to enable the smooth flow of Divine information.

South Africa – Solar Plexus

The whole of South Africa is the solar plexus of the world. And not only is South Africa the solar plexus of the world, but Earth is the solar plexus of the Universe.

We created it so because the Earth is the ultimate litmus test for the Universe. It is the most difficult training ground and, therefore, if it fails in its objective to raise the vibrations of its Souls, under the Veil of Amnesia, this ultimately tells us that Souls do not have the ability to raise their vibrations.

For where is the challenge when you know you are part of Me, of Source?

South Africa is a beautiful country, but a country where the greatest light and the greatest darkness takes place.

Crime, greed, pain and fear are in abundance here, but so is the strength of light and love. There are leaders of light, like Mandela and the hundreds of cutting-edge light-workers working for the betterment of the country. Join them.

Mandela has now Ascended to the ranks of Ascended Masters, and others must follow in his footsteps. Find the Mandela in all of you, the spark of forgiveness. Put kindling to the spark so it lights up your whole life with unconditional love for others. Know your power, know your goodness, and do not shy away from your full potential to contribute to the world through fear and lack of self-confidence. Now is the time to put yourself out there, to strive for a better South Africa, a better world.

South Africa's political leaders have gone astray. Much work must be done by light-workers in the world to put the leaders of South Africa in the energetic light of cleansing. Use the Golden Silver Violet flame, Archangel Gabriel's white light of purification and, of course, use My own energy when you are strong enough to use it – the Source Energy.

There are seven cosmic portals in South Africa and opening these will vastly increase the pace of the Earth's Ascension.

Gobi Desert – Base

A barren wasteland to some, this is the root of the world, the platform upon which she must stand. The people of the Gobi recognise her power and respect the lessons learnt here.

It does require cleansing, but it is not the most unbalanced of the chakras. With some effort and the opening of the portal, there will be a lifting of vibrations and the people of Earth will recognise the support the celestial world always gives them.

Light-workers worldwide should hold the Gobi desert in the light, using the Mahatma Energy and the Source Energy to cleanse and heal it. There are wise light-workers out there who have opened the portal.

Afghanistan – Third Eye

What a mess. It is with much sadness that I behold such a rich country reduced to such base urges and emotions.

It is no coincidence that the country finds itself in such a mess because, as the third eye, it is the centre of confusion and envy.

The psychic dimensions that humans switch off or use for harm are amplified in the third eye.

Afghanistan is sought after not for its resources or location, but for the information held within its soil. Humans do not realise this is what they are fighting for; the land has a natural magnetism.

Afghanistan will not be sorted quickly; it will take many years. But if the other chakras are balanced, the third eye in Afghanistan will follow. If the great portal here can be opened, the speed at which things can be balanced will increase tenfold.

Tibet – Causal

A beautiful and troubled land, but a land that will play an intrinsic role in the world's Ascension. The Dalai Lamas of many incarnations have protected the chakra here, but even their strength has been curtailed by the lack of understanding for the sacredness not just of the Buddhist people, but of the whole of humankind.

Once the Chinese realise this nation's significance to the world, they will reverse the policies that have put them at odds with the people of Tibet and will link arms to protect and balance the chakra.

The causal chakra holds much of the 'baggage' of the world, the intrinsic fears of other races and religions. Once the people of Tibet and China realise there is only one truth, that of *Me*, they will be friends, and then the peoples of the world will unite. This cosmic portal must be opened quickly. Then, life will improve for millions.

Agra, India – Soul Star

The Soul star is in Agra. What a powerful place this is. And yet even though many powerful light-workers reside in Agra, and India more broadly, the country remains off-track and the chakra seriously out of balance.

Much injustice has been done within India, Agra in particular. Much cleansing needs to take place. Put Agra and India in the light, bless them with Archangel Gabriel's white light of purification, and use My own energy, the Source Energy. Bring India and Agra to their full glory.

By opening the portal here, information regarding the connection of humans to the Divine will flow freely through the ley lines of the Earth, and a new dawn will begin.

Fiji – Naval

Fiji, another spectacular creation, and a country blighted by the woes of mankind – not just injustice toward women, but injustices concerning race and greed.

The challenge set has been hard for the people of Fiji and nowhere has it been more acute, by having equal numbers of ethnic Fijians and Indians.

But the people of Fiji are also great. They have great reserves, courage and pride and, together, they will find a path through.

We must hold Fiji in the light; use Archangel Michael's blue light of protection to protect the country from outside influences. Use the Mahatma and Source Energies to cleanse the toxins in the once pure seas, and stand its leaders in the light.

By opening the cosmic portal in Lautoka, Viti Levu, we will bless the land with health and abundance. Once balanced, the naval of the Earth will increase the pace of understanding of the ability to manifest in the physical world. It will also enable men and women to stand equal, enjoying their sexuality but not abusing it.

THE GOLDEN AGE

I f you follow this Manual and perform all the exercises and
visualisations within, you will lift your vibrations such that
you can Ascend. For the world to Ascend and reach the
Golden Age, the world's chakras and portals must be cleared and
energised. You are now ready to play your part in achieving this.

Unlike before, when you Ascend you will not necessarily
pass over. In fact, it is highly unlikely that you will pass over, as
we need Ascended Masters and junior Ascended Masters on the
planet to lift the vibrations of the planet, so have no fear.

Ascension can now happen in the sixth dimension while
you still have much to learn, although you are already powerful light-workers. But you must pass on the information. You
must not proselytise, but you must encourage people to read this
Manual and lift their vibrations.

As I have mentioned, the Golden Age is what we want to
attain. The Golden Age is a shift in what the Earth has been
designed to do.

We will lift the Veil of Amnesia and no longer will people
living on Earth believe they are alone and disconnected from Me.

In the Golden Age, everyone will recognise their link to each
other, to every living thing on the planet and in the Universe.
Most of all, they will recognise that they are created perfectly by

Me, with Me within them, and a part of Me, God, Allah, Source, whatever you choose to call Me. I am One and the Same, always.

In the Golden Age, peace reigns. Everyone has plenty to eat. There is an abundance of joy, of happiness, of music, of laughter, of dancing.

People will still need to learn and it will still be a training ground, but a training ground of advanced Souls, of largely junior Ascended Masters and those nearly there.

It will be a training ground where they must learn to be pure love, and learn the psychic skills assumed in the celestial world. They must learn to be their full higher Souls. They will also learn about other planets, other parts of the Universe, other dimensions.

They will learn how to co-create with the Universe, how to manifest from nothing. And of course, they will learn to embrace their emotions, their sexuality and sensuality. That will remain one of the unique features of the Earth.

In this Golden Age, there will be no more poverty or hunger or fear, no derision or war. There will be peace, love and abundance.

People will live in harmony with nature. They will not exploit nature or live to excess, but they will enjoy a high standard of living. It is a wonderful place to be, the Golden Age. I look upon it with great joy.

I am glad for you because the people reading this book will surely experience it. The people completing this Manual will not only enable the Golden Age, but they will participate in it, either as teachers or pupils.

Reawakening Forgotten Knowledge

In the Golden Age psychic abilities will be commonplace. Have you noticed how more and more channelled publications are available? The wave of social media, of Twitter and Facebook, and other Internet and cellular media are paving the way for a tipping point in spiritual communication? The next leap will be to mainstream psychic abilities – and you, My dear readers, will lead the charge.

The next section will stretch your minds because as humans, most of you have closed your psychic faculties; but as we progress toward the Golden Age, skills like teleportation and levitation will be possible. I ask you to be open to the following section. Enjoy, have fun and awaken the child within you. Awaken the super power within you. The world – *My* world – is magnificent and magical. Be a part of it.

Can You Tele-Transport? How?

Teleportation between different places on the planet or within the Universe was once a common form of transportation. Humans have forgotten how to do this, although this knowledge can be reactivated by modifying the DNA.

The DNA can be modified through a simple auric-level operation, painless and swift. This can be done through visualisation or by asking the celestial realms to intercede.

Particularly specialised Ascended Masters and Archangels able to perform this task are Archangel Raphael and the Prophet Mohammed, although others are also able to do this.

Of course, I can be requested and will then send the necessary messengers. Without making a request, the reprogramming cannot happen. However, if a light-worker is in direct contact with the celestial realms, and works from a position of love and light, celestial beings may instruct that reprogramming should occur for the good of the person and the planet.

Once the DNA reprogramming has been completed (this may take several attempts), the understanding of how to tele-transport is held at a cellular level.

It is now a case of removing the fear and doubt imposed upon humans by the Veil of Amnesia.

How to Reawaken the Knowledge

Relax into a calm meditative state. Tell the body that you wish to reawaken the knowledge of how to teleport for the best and highest path of yourself and the world.

Ask your body to identify the specific nodes that need to be reignited. This could be on the hands, wrists or lower arms.

Identify the place you wish to teleport to and the amount of time you would like to take – teleportation can be immediate, but sometimes bodies can choose to prolong the teleportation period to experience the realm within the shift.

Once the duration and destination have been determined, the body must align with one of Earth's underground and auric level energy lines – only one, e.g. either over or under the ground.

Some of these energy lines are currently blocked, but can be reopened quite easily with the necessary light-work. This may mean it is difficult to teleport within a single room with the physical body, although of course auric transportation – out of body experiences – can be undertaken if the body is unable to align with a specific energy line.

It is not necessary to be at the interconnection of energy lines, but simply on an energy line. The Earth is criss-crossed with such energy lines, and those suitable for teleportation are in a grid system approximately 450m parallel to each other – so squares of grids of approximately 450m.

Therefore, communication to anywhere in the world – as long as the lines are operational – is simple. One may also choose to hop along the same line (teleport along the same line, short distances).

It is not possible to re-materialise inside the body of another being or thing. Therefore, re-materialisation will take place as close as possible to where directions have been set, but outside of other matter.

How to Programme the Specific Location

If you can visualise the place and are confident in where it is, the name, etc., simply repeating the name and visualising it is enough to programme the location into your physical system, which aligns with the Earth's ley line.

If you do not have the exact location, you can use a map form, placing your finger over the destination and thus locking in the destination.

To Lock in the Destination

Before the body can actually teleport, you must lock in the destination. This is done by repeating the name of the destination three times or, if the name isn't known and a map form is being used, by tapping the destination on the map three times and then pressing the modal shift on your hand three times. The modal shift is the node in your hands / wrist / lower arms that needs to be pressed to activate the journey. This may be slightly different on each person and, therefore, should be identified with celestial guidance.

Will Teleportation Need Practice?

Practice will make perfect. Three things are essential for teleportation: 1) reprogramme DNA; 2) reactivate modal shift nodes in the hands / wrists / lower arms; 3) clear energy lines along the Earth's surface.

The Egoic mind can also undermine the body's ability to teleport by challenging the link to the Divine Source of All Things. If the I AM is fully present, then the body knows with full certainty the connection to Source is true, and that Source allows teleportation of matter.

Levitation

Levitation is possible in two main ways: 1) dematerialise the physical body to the point where it is lighter than air and will float; 2) ask to be lifted by celestial beings.

Be open, be committed and be joyful, for you are now entering the place of the mysterious, magical and magnificent, where anything can be achieved.

BECOMING A LIGHT-WORKER

I t is now time for you to take your full place in the world and
its Ascension process – it is time to be a light-worker for Me.
Being a light-worker means you dedicate your life to
the best and highest path of the planet. This does not necessarily
mean renouncing your current job, unless this job has been taken
in the pursuit of greed or power.

It does mean that you actively send out light energy to heal
the world. It also means you recognise that wherever you walk,
each day of your life, you are able to radiate light from your body
and aura, which has a butterfly effect on those around you.

The impact of your light-work, whether through direct contact with people or through the energy you send to heal people,
situations or places, will have an incredible impact and enable the
world to reach its Golden Age.

Light-work is simple, painless and empowering. It is about
your intention and the state of mind you are in when conducting
the work.

A simple example would be that a war has broken out in a
country somewhere in the world. You want to send healing light
and peace to the people of this country.

Light-work would include holding the leaders of this country
in the Golden Silver Violet flame of Archangel Zadkiel, such that

any negative energy they are holding, any fears or negative intentions, are turned to pure positivity. You could also ask Archangel Uriel and his angels of peace and forgiveness to flood through the country.

You may not feel the effect of this, but believe Me: the more people sending healing energy like this, the quicker and more powerful the impact will be.

Similarly, you can decide to heal a person you know or don't directly know, by asking Archangel Raphael to send his angels of healing to that person.

Group light-work is even more powerful, as the vibration of the energy is lifted further by the interaction with others.

The higher the dimension in which you vibrate, the more powerful your light-work will be. This means that for those of you who have reached the seventh dimension, you will be able to co-create with the Universe and manifest intense healing experiences.

For those of you reaching the sixth dimension, your light-work will have the utmost power and be able to shift the outcome of major disruptions and situations.

Those in the fifth dimension will be able to heal people and situations on a smaller, but still significant, scale.

Those of you in the fourth dimension, by deciding to commit your lives to Me and consciously standing in your full power as light-workers, this is enough to enter the fifth dimension. I welcome you with open arms.

I am excited and humbled that so many of you will commit yourselves in service in this way, to the best and highest path of your Self, the planet and the Universe. You are My children and I love you.

⚙ Visualisation ⚙
To Purify Yourself before Light-Work

Ground and protect yourself.

Imagine you are on a beach. You gradually walk into the calm sea in front of you. This is the sea of purification.

You feel the waves wash over your feet and shins. You now walk more deeply into the water, until you are completely submerged by the waves.

Here the salt filters into every cell in your body, cleansing and purifying it, regenerating and reinvigorating it.

As your cells become purified, they glow like gold, until all your body is glistening. At this point, you rise out of the water, like a star, up and up until you reach outer space and join the other stars in the sky.

You now find yourself surrounded by Ascended Masters whom you respect and admire. Jesus asks you to hand over your Ego. You do so willingly. It comes easily through your skin and you hand it to Jesus.

Jesus asks Archangel Zadkiel to stand your Ego in the Golden Silver Violet flame and any negativity within your Ego is turned to pure positivity. Jesus now hands your Ego back to you and it is absorbed into your body.

Jesus holds a golden pink flame in his hand. He places this in your heart chakra. This is the flame of the Christ Consciousness. It is the flame of pure love. Jesus asks you to carry this flame on Earth as you perform your light-work.

He kisses you on your forehead. The other Ascended Masters also kiss your forehead. You feel humbled and empowered. It is now your time to stand in your full power as a light-worker.

When you are ready, continue with your light-work.

Twin Flames and Releasing the Fear of Death

It is now vital to meet your twin flame at an energetic level, in order to release the need for perfection in relationships in this world. This will also help you feel warmth toward death. It is not something to be feared; it is something to be looked forward to, as in death you meet Me, your twin flames, and all your loved ones throughout your lifetimes.

To do light-work, it is important that people release their fear of death. This is because it is one of the deepest fears, and fear blocks the pure energy needed for light-work.

A twin flame is an often-confused term that people use flippantly for a passionate love or ideal partner. In fact, the twin flame is a deeply sacred union. Before all lives, there exists an egg that houses two Souls. These two Souls form the perfect balance of male and female energies. Though these Souls may both take female and male incarnations, they will always return to their original genders at the end of their lives on Earth, and when they have Ascended and joined us in the celestial realm.

Thus it is true that for many who seek the perfect union on Earth, they are actually seeking a return to their home, to their original birth partner, the other Soul that was in the original egg from whence they came.

However, twin flames will not reconnect until both Souls reach the seventh dimension. They will enjoy other extremely important relationships, but the twin flame is reserved for those who have Ascended to full Ascended Master status. The purpose is obvious. For the perfect relationship to be manifested, you need to have learnt the majority of the lessons Earth has to provide you. You cannot find perfect balance, harmony, passion or love unless you have reached this ultimate level of humanity.

Until you have learnt how to love yourself unconditionally and purely, you cannot love another unconditionally and purely. Therefore, the journey to the twin flame is one characterised by challenging relationships, or relationships truly powerful and wonderful but not the 'coming home' that at the deepest level we know we should enjoy.

So for those of you questioning how important it is to pursue the seventh dimension, perhaps this will provide an additional incentive. For if you Ascend to the seventh dimension, and if your twin flame also Ascends to the seventh dimension, you will be reunited. This will be your first reunion since your birth from the egg that carried both your Souls. This is also a written rule because if you could find your twin Soul between lives, you would cease to have a reason to reincarnate.

The union of the twin flame is one of the most uplifting, enriching, completing experiences any Soul can enjoy, other than experiencing the return to Me, which also happens when you enter the seventh dimension. Between lives, there are many training grounds, and there is much time spent with loved ones and friends from countless lives, but not with your twin flame.

People will not be able to meet their twin flames on earth in the sixth dimension, only when they reach the seventh dimension, and even then it will be rare to meet them on Earth. So whilst in *The Lightseeker's Manual* we define Ascension as reaching the sixth dimension – as a special dispensation to you – it will not enable the full lifting of the veil of Amnesia. That will only come with your Ascension to the seventh dimension.

Think of Ascension to the sixth dimension as a level of enlightenment but not the *whole ride*. At an energetic level, people can meet their twin flames whatever the dimension they have reached.

My beloveds, you all have the power to Ascend to the sixth dimension in this lifetime and many of you will reach the seventh dimension. You have My Source Energy, you have the Mahatma Energy, and you have the Golden Silver Violet flame. With these three energies, you can Ascend to the seventh dimension and meet your twin flame. When you know this deep truth, that you are so close to meeting your twin flame, death becomes your friend – not to be looked for prematurely, but when it is time. It is a joyous returning.

With My love, Source, God, Allah, One and the Same.

◎ Visualisation ◎
To Embrace the Golden Age and
Meet Your Twin Flame

You are standing on a bridge. Beneath you runs a golden river. It is the river of humanity, the river of all that is good in humans from across the world. This humanity is what made the most gifted, wise and beneficent individuals who walked the planet: Ascended Masters such as Jesus, Buddha, Mother Mary, Prophet Mohammed, and others.

It is time for you to jump into the river of humanity and become one of the most beneficent humans to exist. It is your time to stand in your full power as an Ascended Master or junior Ascended Master – to know that with your thought and energy, you can change the course of the planet for the better.

You should already have undertaken visualisations for releasing negative ties to places, people and things, as well as the purification ritual. This is your turn to jump, and in doing so, you honour all the best within you – you honour Me and you honour the Divine kingdom. Your Guardian Angel stands beside you as you jump.

Into the river of humanity you fall. As you are submerged beneath its waters, you realise it is the perfect temperature; it is also sweet on your tongue. You easily bob to the surface. It is now your turn to decide whether you want to swim *against* the flow of the river, or *with* it.

In swimming *with* the river, you swim with My guidance; for if you are open to My flow in your life, there will never be any push. It won't be without challenges, but you will always be exactly where you are meant to be.

If you choose to be a light-worker, you choose to serve the best and highest path of your Self, the planet and the Universe. Do you choose this highest path? If so, allow yourself to be carried with your Guardian Angel by the beautiful nurturing current of the river.

You are completely safe, completely held within the warm embrace of the river. Let yourself flow, and as you do, become aware of what passes you on the sides of the river.

What is happening to the world on each side? If you like what you see, give thanks and ask for more. If you want it to change, now is your chance to control the world with your mind.

If you want to use your wings, use them now, for you realise that you have beautiful powerful wings on your back that are ready to unfold. Know that you have full power over the world and your place in it. Any difference from what you choose is because of lessons you need to learn.

As you continue forward, either flying above the river or being carried gently by the current of the river, you arrive at the Golden Age. Here, all is beautiful and the people are happy. Look around you and see what the buildings look like, what the plants and animals look like, what the people are wearing and what they are doing.

When you are ready, climb out of the river. You are perfectly dry and at peace. Find a place where you want to sit in the Golden Age. It is now time for you to meet your friend. This is your twin flame, the other half of the egg from which you were born at the beginning of your time.

That person sits beside you. You feel instantly drawn to them, as though you have known them forever and are now complete. Your twin flame is waiting for you on the other side, as only those in the seventh dimension can be reunited.

The physical world is reserved for your karmic partners, from whom you need to learn and grow. The twin flame is like meeting oneself, for you are born of one. Know that there is nothing to fear in death, for in death you will be reunited with your twin flame.

Talk with your twin flame. Enjoy their company. And when you are ready, thank them and your Guardian Angel and return to the room.

Example of Light-Work
To Heal War

Undertake the visualisation to purify yourself before light-work. Then ask Archangel Uriel to send his legions of angels of peace, forgiveness and love to the war zone.

Imagine golden shimmering light surrounds the country.

Ask for Archangel Zadkiel to stand the whole country in the Golden Silver Violet flame.

Ask Me to send the Source Energy through your body and aura, into the Earth, to heal the planet and this country. The exact words can be as follows:

'I invoke and invite the Archangels, angels, Ascended Masters and Source to heal [this country]. I ask the Source Energy to flow through my body and my aura, into the Earth, healing the Earth and [this country].

'I ask Archangel Uriel: please send your angels of peace and forgiveness to [this country]. Please help them heal, calm and placate the people of [this country], enabling them to forgive and feel unconditional love for each other, and to see the God-spark within each living creature.

'I thank you for your help. So be it, it is done.'

Example of Light-Work
To Heal a Sick or Dying Person

Undertake the visualisation to purify yourself before light-work. Then say:

'I invoke and invite Archangel Raphael to send your angels of healing to [the person]. I ask you to heal them fully and completely, if it is in their best interests for this to be done. I thank you. So be it, it is done.'

Example of Light-Work
To Clear the Earth's Chakras

Undertake the visualisation to purify yourself before light-work. Then say:

'I ask the Archangel Michael to protect me and the [name of chakra and place, e.g. root chakra in the Gobi Desert, China] from all negative energies, toxins, and intentions. I ask that the Source Energy flow through my body and my aura into the Earth, grounding it in the centre of the Earth and radiating this Source Energy back up through the chakra, filling it with multi-coloured light and love energy. I ask that this chakra be purified, healed and energised, for the good of all and the world's Ascension. So be it, it is done. So be it, it is done. So be it, it is done.'

Example of Light-Work to Open a Cosmic Portal

Identify the portal in Table 7 at the end of this Chapter. Undertake the visualisation to purify yourself before light-work. Then say:

'I invoke and invite Archangel Michael to protect me 100% and protect the portal.

'I ask the Archangel Gabriel to pour your beautiful white light of purification through my body and my aura, allowing me to be a pure channel for celestial energy.

'I ask Source: please send your Source Energy through the portal and into my body and my aura, and then into the Earth, allowing the portal to open completely and forever. So be it, it is done.'

Additional Points

In terms of opening portals, remember you must always ask Michael to protect the portal. You must also always use My Source Energy to open the portal.

Your vibrations must also be in the sixth or seventh dimensions to open the portal. It is necessary that you refrain from drinking any alcohol or eating the meat of any living creature (this includes fish) on the day you intend to open a portal. This is because eating meat and drinking alcohol reduces your vibrations.

In some circumstances, the portal will only open in the correct sequence – another portal may require opening first.

For most people, they will need to stand beneath the portal to be able to open it. For this reason, grid references have been provided in this Manual to enable you to locate the portal.

Do let the Channel know when and where you are attempting to open a portal, so she can advise of any guidance I have given her directly.

You may get additional information about opening the portals. Other celestial beings may wish to join you to open the portal, or may specifically need to be involved because of the energy they have.

If you have managed to progress to the stage of light-work with your *energy body*, you may not need to be physically underneath the portal, but may be able to visit with your light-body.

Sometimes it is important to work with other light-workers to open the portal. This is down to how your energies interact in the process.

It is also important to bring information or Divine energy through the portal after it has opened, and push these energies and information out through the ley lines or energy lines of the Earth.

Check with the Channel or contact Me directly. I send love and light to help you open all 99 great cosmic portals.

All 99 require opening by the end of 2016. 40-50 required opening before the end of 2013. This was done. It is the Quest that I bestow upon you light-workers of the world, and I know you are up to the task.

Table 7 The World's 99 Great Cosmic Portals

No.	PLACE	COUNTRY	Location for Light-work[3]
Continental portals			
1	Kabul	Afghanistan	Anywhere in the city
2	Andorra	Andorra	Anywhere in the state
3	South Pole	Antarctic	Anywhere in the Antarctic
4	North Pole	Arctic	Anywhere in the Arctic
5	Eyres Rock, Uluru	Australia	Around or on rock, portal is above rock
6	Mingary	Australia (South)	32.09S 140.46E
7	Carpina	Brazil	7.50S 35.15W
8	Mato Grosso, Chapada de (hills)	Brazil	Anywhere in the state
9	Montes Claros	Brazil	16.45S 43.52W
10	Varginha	Brazil	21.33S 45.25W
11	Meeting Creek, Banff, Alberta	Canada	52.40N 112.42W
12	Helena, New York	Canada, Great Lakes	44.56N 74.43W
13	Ansi	China	40.53N 122.45E
14	Wuhan, Hubei	China	30.35N 114.19E
15	Barranquilla Atlantico	Colombia	11.10N 74.50W

---

3   Where grid references are indicated undertake light-work as close to this point as possible

16	Umangi	Democratic Republic of Congo	2.05N 21.27E
17	The Sphinx,	Egypt	Around base of Sphinx
18	The Giza Pyramid	Egypt	Around base of pyramid or within
19	Luxor Temple	Egypt	Within grounds
20	Reid Abdair	Ethiopia	7.22N 44.32E
21	Lautoka	Fiji	Anywhere in the Fijian archipelago
22	Montague de Aigoual	France	44.08N 3.35E
23	St Fargeau	France	47.38N 3.04E
24	St Gaultier	France	46.38N 1.26E
25	Saint-Merd-la-Breuille	France	45.44N 2.26E
26	Saale Talsperre, Bleilochsperre	Germany	50.29N 11.43E
27	St Claude	Guadaloupe W.I	16.02N 61.42W
28	Guatemala/Honduras	Guatemala	Along the border
29	Honolulu	Hawaii	Anywhere in the city
30	Adegaon	India	22.37N 79.32E
31	Saran, Bihar	India	24.29N 86.19E
32	Hyderabad	India	Anywhere in the city
33	The Ganges (Source)	India	Anywhere at the headwaters
34	Varanasi	India	Anywhere in the city

35	Taj Mahal, Agra	India	In front of the Taj Mahal (portal directly above highest point of the Taj)
36	Aliambata	Indonesia	8.48S 126.34E
37	Tokamachi	Japan	37.08N 138.44E
38	Tsuruoka	Japan	38.42N 139.50E
39	Nura	Kazakhstan	48.32N 74.01E
40	Yangibazar	Kyrgyzstan	41.38N 70.54E
41	Bamako	Mali	Above the great mosque
42	Mongolia	Mongolia	Anywhere in the country
43	Gobi Desert	Mongolia	Anywhere in the Gobi desert
44	Porirua East	New Zealand	41.08S 174.53E
45	Altafjord inet	Norway	70.10N 23.00E
46	Bermuda Triangle	Pacific Ocean	Attempt only with light-body, not physically
47	Lago Titicaca	Peru	Anywhere on the lake
48	Machu Picchu	Peru	Within the Temple of the sun
49	Manila	Philippines	Anywhere in the city
50	Faddeya, Mys	Russia	62.40N 179.43E
51	Agata	Russia	66.56N 93.30E
52	Omsk	Russia	Anywhere in Omsk
53	Gora Chen	Russia	Anywhere on or at the base of the mountain 65.25N 141.45E (portal directly above)

54	Opala	Russia	51.58N 156.30E
55	Tshohoha Nord L	Rwanda	Anywhere in Rwanda
56	Al Fayd	Saudi Arabia	18.01 N 43.42E
57	Mecca	Saudi Arabia	
58	Yaaqle	Somalia	2.26N 45.25E
59	Knysna Forest	South Africa	Anywhere within forest
60	Wonderboom	South Africa	Anywhere in the town
61	Lion's Head, Cape Town	South Africa	On the summit
62	Alconchel	Spain	38.31.N 7.04W
63	Pissevache	Switzerland	46.08N 7.00E
64	Chon Buri	Thailand	13.24N 100.59E
65	Ankor Wat	Thailand	Within grounds
66	Potala Palace, Lassa, Dalai Lama's residence before exile	Tibet	Close to the Potala Palace (portal is directly above the palace)
67	Gundogdu, Rize	Turkey	41.03N 40.38E
68	Stone Henge	United Kingdom	Close to the circle, portal is directly above
69	Bathpool, Cornwall	United Kingdom	From the bridge or beside the river
70	*City* of London	United Kingdom	Within the old city walls marked by Aldgate, Bishops Gate, Ludgate and Moorgate
71	York	United Kingdom	By the cathedral

72	Ramapo Mts, New York, New Jersey	USA	Anywhere along mountain range
73	Rock Island, Illinois	USA	41.30N 90.34W
74	Alaska	USA	Anywhere in the state
75	Sedona	USA	34.53N 111.45W
76	Ribat	Yemen	14.22N 44.30E

Oceanic portals

77	Sea off coast of Marseilles, France	Mediterranean Sea	From the shoreline
78	Atlantis	Atlantic Ocean	31 15'15.53N, 24 15'30.53W
79	Sea off West Coast of Canada	North Pacific Ocean	55N 31.39W
80	Sea off East Coast of New Zealand	South Pacific Ocean	45S 165W
81	Sea off East Coast of Mexico	Gulf of Mexico	23.36N 91.60W
82	Sea of UK	North Sea	54.34N 11.50E
83	Sea near Jan Mayen island, Norway	North Atlantic Ocean	71.30N 9.00E
84	Sea off Australia	Coral Sea	17.40S 153E
85	Sea off Antarctica	Southern Ocean	63S 172.36E

Stellar portals

86	Canis Minor, Procyon	Equatorial zone	Identify visual image of the constellation. Undertake light-work at night. Direct healing energy towards the sky/location of the constellation. Light-worker can be located anywhere on Earth to open/energise stellar portals, but intention upon specific portal must be clear.
87	Pegasus	Equatorial zone	
88	Zubenelgenubi, Libra	Equatorial zone	
89	Leo Minor	Equatorial zone	
90	South Galactic Pole, Sculptor	Southern sky	
91	Pictor	Southern sky	
92	Virgo	Southern sky	
93	Draco	Northern sky	
94	Bootes	Northern sky	
95	Ophiuchus	Equatorial zone/northern sky	
96	Cepheus	Northern sky	
97	Equuleus	Northern sky	
98	Pisces	Northern sky	
99	Perseus	Northern sky	

Conclusion and Prayer of the Ascended Masters

Peace be upon you, My beloved children, for My kingdom is now yours to bring to Earth. You have now completed the Manual.

For those of you who have taken the time to perform all the exercises and visualisations, you will have Ascended to at least the fifth dimension.

For those of you who have been using the Source Energy and Mahatma Energy regularly, as well as the Golden Silver Violet flame, you will be in the sixth dimension.

Some of you will have Ascended to full Ascended Master status and be in the seventh dimension, although still with the Veil of Amnesia. Many of you will be communicating easily and powerfully with the celestial world, My angels, Ascended Masters and other celestial beings.

You have entered the realm of the Magnificent and the magical. Know your full power and use it for the world. Be a light-worker and stand in your full power.

I will now give you a prayer that you should use every day, when you start the day and when you finish it. It should ideally be said while standing, with feet hip-width apart and shoulders back, to feel your full power. This is the prayer of the Ascended Masters.

Daily Prayer

I [your name] stand before you an Ascended Master in my full power. I AM healed, I AM love, I AM power for the good of the world and the Universe. I stand a part of my Monad, with you, Source, within me.

I stand as a light-worker, committing my life in service to the Divine. I stand embracing the power to co-create with the Universe, to carry the Christ Consciousness, and to be equal to the angels in our commitment and glory of your Light.

I now choose to manifest the Golden Age on this Earth. I choose to release all negativity and replace it with positivity, as the central tenet of my life.

I choose to embrace the new technologies and psychic abilities you bestow upon me.

I share my love and light with the world, with every person, the birds, animals, and creatures of the planet, the fish and the trees. I embrace all and dedicate myself to healing the planet, and protecting the abundance of Lady Gaia.

So be it, it is done.

So be it, it is done

So be it, it is done.

Example Timetable for Weeks 21 and 22

Activity	Week 21							Week 22						
	1	2	3	4	5	6	7	1	2	3	4	5	6	7
Ground and protect yourself every day. Use the Golden Silver Violet flame and the Source or Mahatma Energy every day.														
Undertake the visualisation to purify before light-work. This must be undertaken before you do any light-work.														
Undertake the visualisation: Embrace the Golden Age and Meet Your Twin Flame.														
Send Light to heal a person, place, or thing.														
Undertake light-work to cleanse a chakra – choose a single chakra or more than one.														
Identify a great cosmic portal near to you that you can visit to open or cleanse.														
Prayer of the Ascended Masters (daily).														

Epilogue – by Helena Clare

You have now completed the Manual. I hope the journey has been magnificent for you. If you have questions, please contact me on my website www.LightseekersWay. com. I've also posted some further reading up there, if you want to probe more into working with the angels or with energy fields.

Since I began channelling this Manual at the end of 2011, there has already been a shift in the trajectory of the Earth. At the turn of 2012, Source channelled that the end of the world was a possibility within the year if major strides weren't taken. Due to the light-work undertaken in that year, the world did not end. Even more moving is the message I received that Earth is now on a trajectory where it can reach the Golden Age. This message has been received from the celestial realms by a number of light-workers globally.

However, from the pages you have read, you will see that the Earth is not yet out of the danger zone and recent events with Covid demonstrate the path is not smooth. Please don't underestimate the power all of you have through reading this Manual and undertaking the exercises and visualisations. The celestial realm is desperate to help us, but they need to be asked, for we, as a race, have free will. So connect with your angels, ground and protect yourselves every day, use the energies – the Christ Consciousness,

Golden Silver Violet flame, the Mahatma and Source Energies – and we all can bring about the Golden Age, smoothly and swiftly.

I hope you have also progressed closer to you ultimate potential, the **I AM** that is within you. Love yourself. Take a risk if your intuition and guidance tells you to. In that way, you will fulfil your full potential.

Lastly, one of the major purposes of *The Lightseeker's Manual* is to give you the grid coordinates for the major cosmic portals in the world, so you can beam your light and love to these portals and open them. The world needs *you*. There are many portals, and all need opening.

At the time of writing and working with other light-workers, I have been privileged to be involved in opening 11 great portals. It is a mysterious and magnificent experience to open a portal, and working with other light-workers is fun and rewarding. Be part of the wave of change. Open a great cosmic portal, or even a smaller portal. And if you plan to or have already done so, please let me know so I can keep track of our work on the website.

Since I've committed my life fully in service to the Divine, life hasn't become easier, but in some ways it makes more sense. Events seem to unfurl (when I'm not trying to fight against them) in an organic, natural way. But for me, the most significant part of working with the angels and Source for so many years, including the work I've done on my own issues, is that I remain happy despite the tumult around me.

I love chocolate. Until the last few years, I would describe my happiness like one of those hollow chocolate Easter eggs: my life looked good, but I felt empty inside. Now my happiness is like a rich Belgian praline chocolate, rich and full at the centre, whole and complete.

It's been a tough journey and it's not over, but I know I'm looked after and blessed in so many ways. I thank the celestial kingdom for the opportunity to be on Earth at this time and to have such beautiful, loving beings entwined with my life.

I wish you love, abundance and fulfilment on your journey toward the Light.

Glossary

Affirmation – a spoken, written or thought statement of intent.

Angel – beings of pure love, messengers of Source (God), without free will. They pursue God's will, always for the good of the Universe. They have rarely incarnated in human form.

Archangel – senior angels, they lead thousands of angels.

Ascended Masters – evolved humans who have reached the seventh dimension. They always retain some Ego and have free will, even in the seventh dimension. They possess pure love and are committed to the good of the world and the Universe.

Ascension – enlightenment; when a human evolves to the level of at least a junior Ascended Master (sixth dimension) and is not required to reincarnate on Earth again.

Aura – the energetic field around the physical body.

Celestial being – beings who reside in the seventh dimension and work closely with Source.

Chakras – energy centres within the body and aura.

Christ Consciousness Energy – the energy of pure love that Jesus brought to Earth.

Dimensions – a term used to denote the stages through which a human passes to reach Ascension.

Gateways – entry and exit points for moving through the Earth's aura at great distances and speeds.

God-spark – the pure essence of God that runs through every living creature.

Golden Age – where all on the planet share in peace, prosperity, freedom and health and live in harmony with nature and the animal kingdom. All humans in the Golden Age will be in at least the fifth dimension.

Golden Silver Violet flame – a powerful celestial energy that turns all negativity to positivity.

Great cosmic portals – energy doorways in the Earth's aura that must be opened to allow an abundance of Divine energy and information.

Great Divine Director – Chair of the Karmic Panel, who holds the blueprint of all human Souls.

Grounding – the ritual of imagining a connection to the core of the Earth.

I AM – the 'I AM' prefix to a statement, e.g. 'I AM healed', is a human's identification with this highest part within themselves. Saying the 'I AM', brings them closer to this state of being.

Karma – the balance of good deeds and bad deeds.

Karmic Panel – the panel that assesses the balance of good and bad deeds after a human's death.

Levitation – the ability to lift and hold oneself away from the Earth.

Light-Worker – a person dedicated to serving the greatest good of the planet, and actively using their energies and powers to heal the world.

Light-Body – the energetic part of a human, as opposed to the physical body; the aura.

Lords of Karma – celestial beings on the Karmic Panel who assess a Soul's karma at the end of each life. They are seventh-dimensional beings of pure love.

Mahatma Energy – a powerful celestial energy that Mahatma Ghandi brought to Earth. It has many qualities, including healing toxins and disease and increasing the pace of spiritual growth, if used for the benefit of the user and Earth.

Meditation – an exercise where a human seeks to relax and clear the mind.

Monad – also known as the Soul Group, the Monad comprises 12 Souls. One Soul always remains with Source. The other 11 Souls go into the Universe to experience.

Orb – the energy of celestial beings that can be captured on camera.

Protection – the ritual of asking for celestial protection for the mind, body and spirit – for instance, from Archangel Michael.

Seventh dimension – the level where celestial beings of pure love reside.

Soul – each Soul is comprised of 12 Soul Aspects. One Soul Aspect always remains with the Soul, while the other 11 go out and experience.

Source Energy – Source's own energy and the most powerful energy ever to be gifted to Earth.

Teleportation – the ability to move from one place to another instantaneously.

Twin Flame – two Souls born of one egg. The twin flame of a person is the other Soul to be born from this egg at the beginning of the Souls' incarnations. When both Souls have Ascended to the seventh dimension, they will be reunited. Twin flames cannot meet in the physical realm or between lives before they have both Ascended to the seventh dimension. They are the perfect balance of male and female energies – the yin-yang balance.

Veil of Amnesia – the state where humans forget their connection to Source and the celestial kingdom when they incarnate on Earth, and one reason why Earth is a particularly challenging place to incarnate

Vibrations – the frequency of light at which beings vibrate. Source vibrates fastest of all.

Visualisation – an inner journey using pictures, like a film in your mind.

Acknowledgements

I acknowledge with joy and love:
Source and the celestial beings who have made my life such a rich adventure; who have nurtured me and guided me unfalteringly; and who have gifted us this book.

My mum, dad, sister and brother for making the sun shine. My beautiful children for the love and inspiration they radiate to me everyday.

The wonderful healers who have defined my life's journey and taught me so much. Tessa, with whom the journey began. Marie, Mette and Anthea, great Ka Hunas who taught me about the power of touch. Verona, one of the most cutting edge light-workers globally; and Margi of the Angel Connection School, whose practical, no-nonsense love and guidance helped my angelic connection leap forward, and whose friendship remains a rock. Eric, Wendy, Lisa and Piet for the partnership in light-work. Wendy, Toni, Shameela, and my sister Sarah for their comments on the first draft and their love and encouragement.

Stephanie and her team for professional guidance and brilliance in publishing *The Lightseeker's Manual*. Renee and Lewis for their amazing illustrations!

All my friends, family and greatest critics – for making my life miraculous.

About Helena Clare

Raised in Cornwall UK, at the foot of Bodmin moor, at age 18, Helena took a year out from studying to teach English at a university in Kalimantan, on the Indonesian part of the rainforest island of Borneo. The experience influenced her life, both through witnessing the degradation caused by profligate logging and being exposed to the psychic abilities and experiences of the students whom she taught and who befriended her, resonating with her own ability to converse with celestial beings.

Upon her return to England she studied a Bachelor of Science in Economics at the London School of Economics and then received a scholarship to study a Masters in Environmental Economics, at University College London. After graduating with distinction she took up a joint post in Fiji, as Senior Natural Resource Advisor in the Fiji Mineral Resources Department and the South Pacific Applied Geoscience Commission. In this role she supported governments in the Pacific to develop sustainable mineral and natural resource policies. At the same time she began training to be a Ka Huna masseur, a deep spiritual massage from

Hawaii, that can release emotions trapped in the body, from this life and previous lives.

After two years in the Pacific Helena returned to London and took a position with the UK government's aid department, the Department for International Development, where she spent the next twelve years. Under Clare Short's leadership the department set the benchmark for innovation and reform in the international aid and trade architecture, to be more inclusive of less well-off countries and to benefit the poorest people in the world.

After contributing to critical trade agendas including the relaxation of intellectual property rights on life savings drugs, she was posted to South Africa. Here she met her first husband and continued her career in trade, regional economic development and finding solutions for climate change challenges, designing and leading multi-million pound initiatives aimed at improving the lives of millions of the poorest people in Africa and globally.

Whilst in South Africa she studied kinesiology, a practice that uses the body's innate knowledge to heal itself, and qualified as an Angel and Ascension Teacher with the Angel Connection School. In December 2012 Helena began channelling *The Lightseeker's Manual*. Since then she has also published *The Spiritual Side of Disability – The Lightseeker's Way to Thrive with a Special Needs Child* and *Spirit Baby - Communicate with your unborn baby. Ease your birth*. She has also continued her career as an international development leader.

She is mum to two beautiful boys, Tariq and Saafi, who are her delight and joy. She has dedicated her life to finding solutions to the world's most critical challenges, as well as empowering people to find their own *highest paths*. She lives with her two sons and shares her time between South Africa and the UK.

Free Printable PDFs

To help you get the most out of your Lightseeker's Manual journey, Helena has set up a special webpage where you can download printable PDFs. Here's what you'll receive:

- Table 1   Chakra Characteristics in the Seventh Dimension
- Table 2   Celestial Beings for the Heart Chakra
- Table 3   Ascended Masters, Qualities and Retreats
- Table 4   The Human Energy Field and Chakras in the Fifth Dimension
- Table 5   Ailment Chart
- Table 6   The World's Chakras and Celestial Guardians
- Table 7   The World's 99 Great Cosmic Portals
- Worksheets for Weeks 1 - 22 of the Velocity Ascension manual

To get your free PDFs go to:
Lightseekersway.com/freepdfs

CONNECT ON SOCIAL MEDIA
Twitter: Helena Clare @LightseekersWay
Facebook: The Lightseeker's Way
Instagram: helenaclare.lightseekersway
Website: www.LightseekersWay.com

CONTACT HELENA
Contact Helena about speaking engagements, media appearances
or just to say hello at www.LightseekersWay.com
and email helena@lightseekersway.com

CPSIA information can be obtained
at www.ICGtesting.com
Printed in the USA
LVHW080503090222
710484LV00017BA/2140